Portraits

of

Asian-Pacific Americans

By
Kim Sakamoto Steidl

Illustrated by Franz Steidl

Cover by Franz Steidl

Copyright © Good Apple, 1991

ISBN No. 0-86653-598-5

Printing No. 987654321

Good Apple
1204 Buchanan St., Box 299
Carthage, IL 62321-0299

S I M O N   &   S C H U S T E R   *A Paramount Communications Company*

Table of Contents

GA1323

GA1323

Dedication

This book is dedicated to
those first immigrants
who opened the path
for future generations

and

my family
for their
love, encouragement and practical assistance.

Acknowledgements

This book would not have been possible without these individual and institutional contributors:

Jan Allianic	Sandy Lydon	Amateur Athletic Association
Helen Brown	Mary Ann Mateo	Japanese American Curriculum Project
Myra Lynn Cortado	Dave Moore	Korea Times
Fred Hattori	Jeanne Nakano	National Japanese American Historical Society
Joe Hattori	Malathai Narayan	Steidl/Younger Design Associates
Shirley Ito	Suzie Oh	UCLA Asian Studies Center
Jim Kahune	Angelina Ongkeko	USC Library
Jane Kim	Tara Sethia	Visual Communications
Lisa Kim	Amy Tan	
Sox Kitashima	Meg Thornton	
Disa Lindgren	Bill Watanabe	

In Memory
of
Senator Spark Matsunaga

GA1323

Teacher Notes

We can learn so much from the personal stories of others. The biographies provided in this book represent a cross section of Asian-Pacific Americans. Their life experiences are intended to inspire and give examples of the great diversity that exists in the Asian-Pacific American community.

By recognizing the achievements and contributions of Americans from all backgrounds, we can hopefully gain a clearer understanding of our collective American heritage.

This book is intended to be used as a supplement to the teacher's existing curriculum. As teachers we can facilitate a better understanding of the world we live in by first recognizing and addressing our own biases, and then presenting materials that reflect accurate and positive images of all groups. By addressing prejudice and discrimination openly with our students, we are able to foster an awareness and sensitivity towards others thus underscoring the principles established by the founders of our great nation.

GA1323

The Pacific Rim

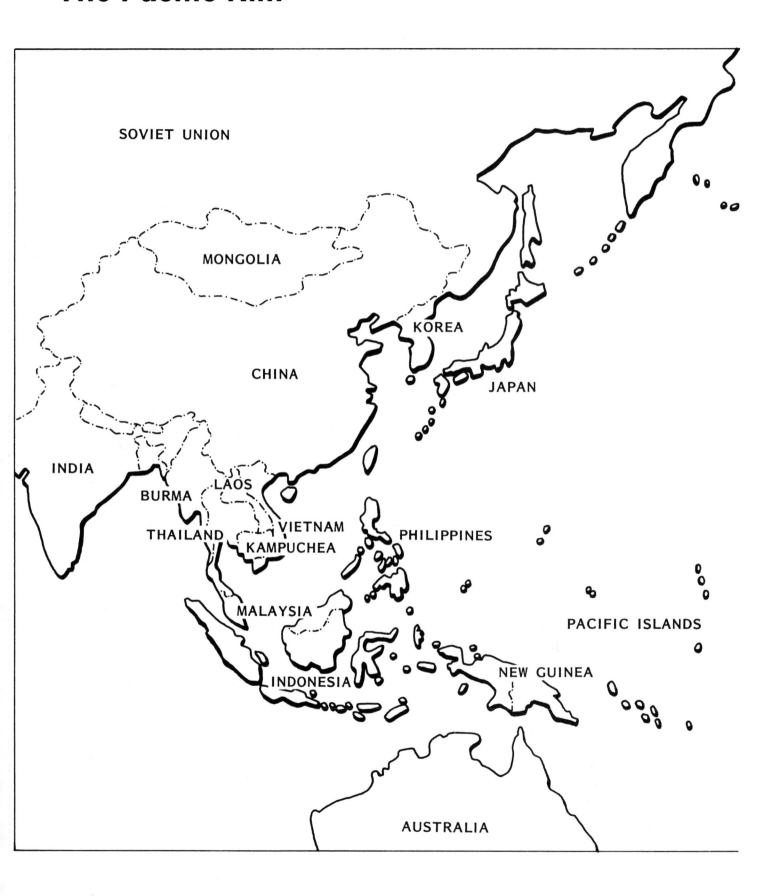

SOVIET UNION

MONGOLIA

CHINA

KOREA

JAPAN

INDIA

LAOS

BURMA

VIETNAM

THAILAND

KAMPUCHEA

PHILIPPINES

MALAYSIA

PACIFIC ISLANDS

INDONESIA

NEW GUINEA

AUSTRALIA

GA1323

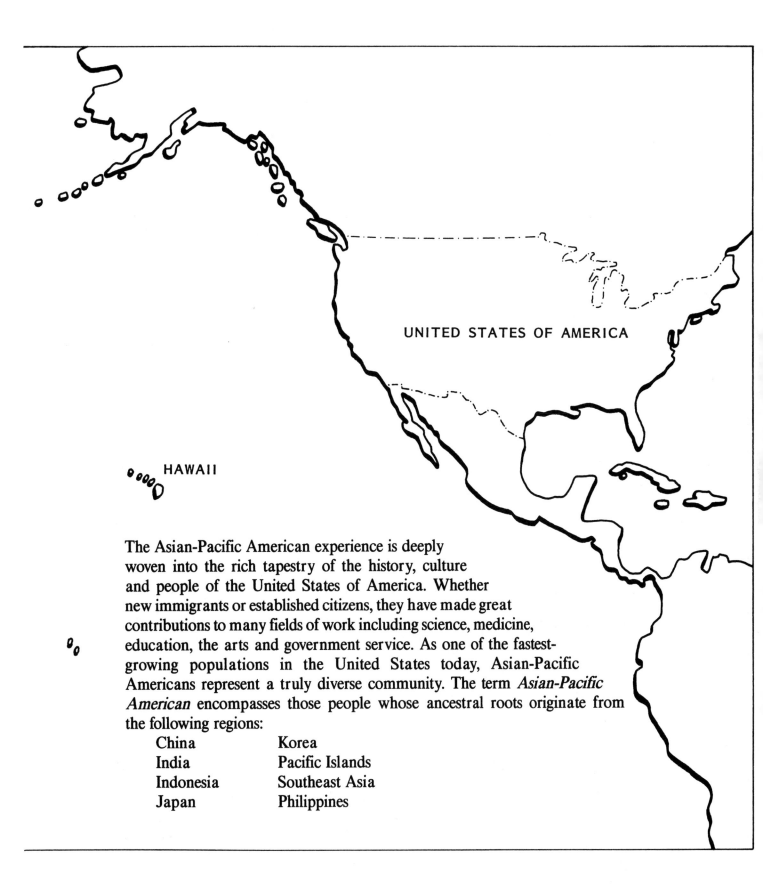

UNITED STATES OF AMERICA

HAWAII

The Asian-Pacific American experience is deeply
woven into the rich tapestry of the history, culture
and people of the United States of America. Whether
new immigrants or established citizens, they have made great
contributions to many fields of work including science, medicine,
education, the arts and government service. As one of the fastest-
growing populations in the United States today, Asian-Pacific
Americans represent a truly diverse community. The term *Asian-Pacific
American* encompasses those people whose ancestral roots originate from
the following regions:

China	Korea
India	Pacific Islands
Indonesia	Southeast Asia
Japan	Philippines

ACTIVITY
Who Are Asian-Pacific Americans?

The United States census lists the following Asian-Pacific American groups living in America today:

Asian Americans

Chinese	Burmese	Pakistani	Indo-Chinese
Filipino	Cambodian (Kampuchean)	Sri Lankan	Iwo Jiman
Japanese	Hmong	Thai	Javanese
Asian Indian	Indonesian	Bhutanese	Maldivian
Korean	Laotian	Borneo	Nepalese
Vietnamese	Malayan	Celebesian	Sikkimese
Bangladeshi	Okinawan	Cernan	Singaporean

Pacific Islanders

Polynesian (Hawaiian, Samoan, Tahitian, Tongan and Tokelauan)
Micronesian (Guamanian, Saipanese, Tinian Islander, Mariana Islander, Marshallese and Palauan)
Melanesian (Fiji, Papua New Guinean, Solomon Islander and New Hebrides Islander)

TEAMWORK IN GEOGRAPHY

Using the census list above, see how many countries and islands you can locate on a detailed world map or globe. Work in teams of two or three. Fill out a fact card (index cards can also be used) for each area you locate. Get together with other teams and quiz each other on the information you have collected.

Fact Card

Name of country or island:

How far away is it from the U.S. mainland?
(Use San Francisco as a locating point.)

What are the major bodies of water surrounding it?

What are the closest or bordering countries?

List three unique features of the country or island by looking only at a map or a globe.

4

GA1323

Events in Asian-Pacific American History
Chinese Americans

1769 The Spanish explorer Portolá comes upon a village near present day Los Angeles, California, believed to be founded by Chinese who worked as shipbuilders between 1571 and 1746 in Baja, California. The village was called by the Chinese name "Yangna."

1848 Economic depression in China and the discovery of gold in California bring the first significant numbers of Chinese to America. Thousands are also drawn to Hawaii by the promise of work in the sugarcane fields.

1869 The Transcontinental Railroad is completed. Under harsh working conditions, Chinese workers contribute significantly to the completion of the western section. Railroad workers leave to find jobs in the West and other parts of the United States. Anti-Chinese violence and sentiments intensify.

1882 The Chinese Exclusion Act halts Chinese immigration to the United States and prevents Chinese already here from becoming naturalized citizens. This law will be repealed in 1943.

1948 The Displaced Persons Act allows for the more than 3500 Chinese visiting and working in the United States since the outbreak of the Chinese Civil War to have permanent resident status. This event begins the second major wave of immigration to the United States that still continues today.

1952 The McCarran-Walter Act allows for immigrants from Asian and the Pacific Islands to become United States citizens.

1978 Large numbers of Chinese from Southeast Asia emigrate to the United States to escape the war.

1980 The United States census finds 805,000 people of Chinese ancestry living in the United States.

1989 The student protest in Beijing's Tiananmen Square and the following repression bring political refugees from China.

Connie Chung
Television Journalist

Connie Chung is one of the best known journalists in television. She is well liked by her audience and respected by her colleagues in broadcasting. The secret to her success is just plain hard work.

Connie was born and raised in Washington, D.C. Her father worked for the United Nations, and her mother was a homemaker. She started her career as a secretary for a local Washington TV station, with hopes of becoming a newswriter. She got her chance. Whenever a new story came into the station, Connie volunteered to cover it. She gained valuable experience and was soon sent to cover major stories like the 1972 Nixon-McGovern presidential campaign and the Watergate hearings. She developed a reputation for being tenacious and a tough interviewer.

Connie is now involved with several television projects at one time. In addition to anchoring the CBS nightly news, she has also hosted her own prime time TV shows and special reports. The shows' topics range from interviewing celebrities to reporting current findings on stress and aging.

In 1987 Connie visited China for the first time. She met her relatives and talked with them about how World War II and China's Cultural Revolution affected their family. She found the experience very rewarding and gained an understanding of her heritage and herself.

Connie Chung is a trailblazer. She was one of the first Asian-Pacific American women on national television. Her professionalism, intelligence and sincerity before the camera are just a few reasons why she has become one of the nation's leading television journalists.

TELEVISION NEWS MAKERS

Television viewers are accustomed to seeing the news appear like magic every evening. Yet for each report many hours of research, writing and editing are required. More and more the people assembling the news themselves represent the diversity of our country. In front of the cameras are the anchors and reporters who inform us about the main events of the day. Behind the scenes they are supported by producers, directors, camera operators, engineers, art directors and more who make sure that the news gets on the air.

There are a number of prominent Asian-Pacific Americans in broadcast journalism.

Wendy Tokuda gained her reputation as a news anchor for Channel 5 Eyewitness News, San Francisco. She has also produced her own award-winning series *Tokuda Reports.*

Wynette Yao is an ABC News production associate. She was a contributor to the documentary *Faces of History* which examined the history of Asian-Pacific Americans.

David Louie is a veteran reporter who has been in the business for over twenty years. He has been recognized for his volunteerism in the Asian-Pacific American community.

David Liu is an Emmy award-winning producer. He is also a founding member of the National Asian American Telecommunications Association.

Ken Kashiwahara is a network correspondent and bureau chief for ABC news. He is well-known for his news coverage of national and world news.

ACTIVITY
Connie Chung
Television Journalist
TV NEWSCASTING

Produce a television news broadcast. Get together with some friends and select the following:

- news anchors (in studio)
- reporters (remote broadcasts, on location)
- camera crew (in studio and on location)
- news director
- sports announcer (optional)
- weatherman or woman (optional)

Some of you may hold more than one job. Send your reporters out in the classroom, or out into the school, and gather newsworthy events. Have your news director (or editor) check the reports and talk them over with the anchors. Select the best stories and put them on the air.

This activity can be as simple or complex as you like. It could be a simple skit with three or four of your friends or a thorough project that might take hours to put together. Perhaps you can obtain a video camera to tape the project and play it back to your class. You may use props (channel number, desks, weather map), dress up, tape sports activities at school or just make it a humorous spoof with two or three friends.

7

Asian-Pacific Americans in Sports

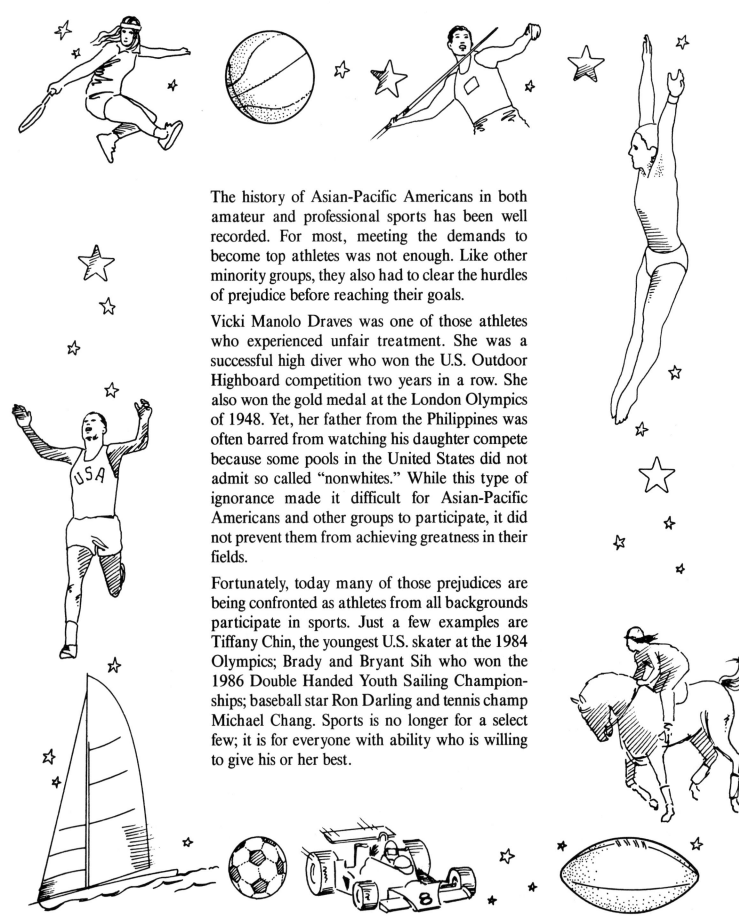

The history of Asian-Pacific Americans in both amateur and professional sports has been well recorded. For most, meeting the demands to become top athletes was not enough. Like other minority groups, they also had to clear the hurdles of prejudice before reaching their goals.

Vicki Manolo Draves was one of those athletes who experienced unfair treatment. She was a successful high diver who won the U.S. Outdoor Highboard competition two years in a row. She also won the gold medal at the London Olympics of 1948. Yet, her father from the Philippines was often barred from watching his daughter compete because some pools in the United States did not admit so called "nonwhites." While this type of ignorance made it difficult for Asian-Pacific Americans and other groups to participate, it did not prevent them from achieving greatness in their fields.

Fortunately, today many of those prejudices are being confronted as athletes from all backgrounds participate in sports. Just a few examples are Tiffany Chin, the youngest U.S. skater at the 1984 Olympics; Brady and Bryant Sih who won the 1986 Double Handed Youth Sailing Championships; baseball star Ron Darling and tennis champ Michael Chang. Sports is no longer for a select few; it is for everyone with ability who is willing to give his or her best.

GA1323

Michael Chang

Tennis Pro

At age 15 Michael Chang became the youngest player ever to win the United States Junior Tennis Championship. That was the same year he turned professional. Michael is one of the most promising stars in the world of tennis. Some believe that he will reach the level of such tennis greats as John McEnroe and Bjorn Borg. At 5'9" and weighing 139 pounds, he is known for his strong topspin forehand and intense on-court concentration.

Michael was born in Hoboken, New Jersey, in 1972. His father and older brother Carl taught him tennis basics when he was just six years old. Two years later he won his first junior tournament. He progressed so fast that it was hard to find the right coach to match his skills. Michael had

very little time for friends and leisure activities. Instead, he chose to work on improving his game. He says, "Anytime you want to be the best at something, you have to sacrifice something."

Since his win at the French Open in 1989, Michael has also learned about another aspect of success— celebrity status. However, he has grown used to the photo sessions, autograph signing and commercial endorsements.

Throughout his career Michael has felt a deep sense of gratitude toward his family for supporting him every step of the way. He is very proud of them and the fact that they are Chinese Americans.

ACTIVITY
Michael Chang
Tennis Pro
RULES OF THE GAME

Pick your favorite sport and briefly discuss it.

1. Name of sport: _____

2. How many can play (are on the team)? _____

3. What kind of equipment is needed? _____

   _____

4. What kind of location or facility is required? _____

   _____

5. Briefly describe how the game is played and some of the rules. _____

   _____

   _____

   _____

   _____

   _____

   _____

6. Why do you like this sport? _____

   _____

   _____

   _____

   _____

   _____

GA1323

ACTIVITY

Asian-Pacific Americans in Sports
CREATE YOUR OWN SPORTS WORD SEARCH

Make a word search puzzle by hiding words from the field of sports.

You can write your words horizontally, vertically, diagonally or in reverse order. Use all capital letters. Fill in the blank spaces with random letters.

Write your words below the word search grid.

When you are finished, give your paper to a friend to try and solve it.

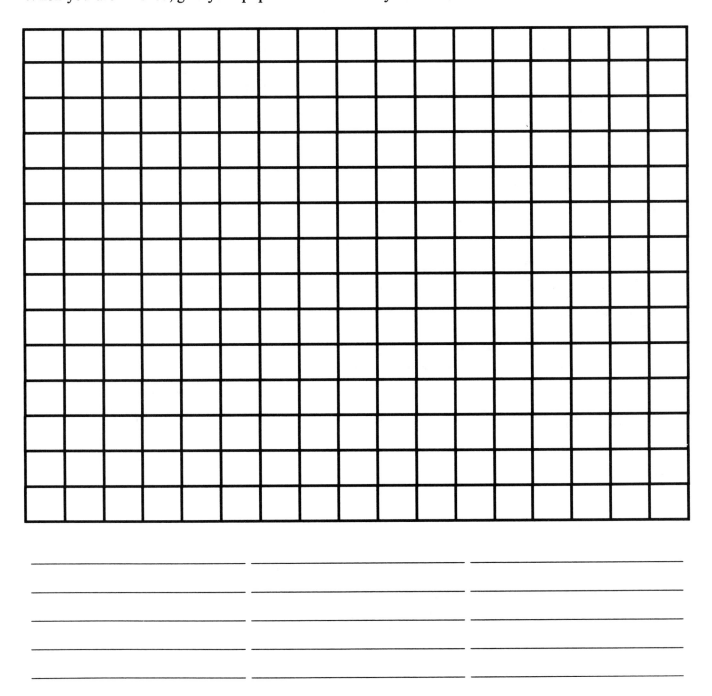

_____   _____   _____

_____   _____   _____

_____   _____   _____

_____   _____   _____

_____   _____   _____

GA1323

Asian-Pacific American Architects

There are many outstanding Asian-Pacific Americans in the field of architecture. The role of the architect is to create a structure that is both useful and beautiful.

Ieoh Ming Pei is one of the foremost architects of our time. His work is known throughout the world. His style is to design buildings that fit into the surroundings of the city. The glass and metal pyramid in the Louvre in Paris and the tallest building in Los Angeles are just two of his structures.

Maya Ying Lin is the architecture student who designed the Vietnam War Memorial in Washington, D.C. The two smoothly polished granite walls, one pointing to the Washington Monument and the other to the Lincoln Memorial, are a tribute to veterans and the more than fifty thousand soldiers who died in the Vietnam War.

Minoru Yamasaki is the architect of the world's tallest buildings, the over-one-hundred story twin towers of the World Trade Center in New York City. He is recognized as a leader in modern architectural design.

Worley K. Wong is known for his ability to place his structures in harmony with their environment. He has been active in professional groups such as the State of California's Board of Architectural Examiners and the National Council of Architectural Registration Boards.

ACTIVITY

Asian-Pacific American Architects
ENVIRONMENTAL ARCHITECTURE

Design a building or structure that takes people and the environment into consideration. Consider the following:

- Location (city, park, country, beach, etc.)
- Materials (natural materials like rocks, wood, etc., and others like concrete, steel, glass, etc.)
- Purpose (designed for people to work in, for recreation, for both, for shopping, etc.)
- Environmental Impact: What will the building do to the existing land? (Will you have to take over parts of nature, cut trees, bulldoze?) How much traffic will the building create? How will the building fit into the surrounding area?
- Special Considerations: Will there be access for differently abled (disabled) people?
- Style: Will the style of architecture fit in with the style of surrounding buildings?

Draw a floor plan of the building and a side view.

Maya Ying Lin
Architecture Student

Out of 1400 entries for the Vietnam War Memorial, Maya Ying Lin's design was chosen. Her design of a black granite wall etched with the names of 58,000 men and women who sacrificed their lives in Vietnam honestly depicted the harsh reality of war. A student of architecture at Yale University, twenty-year-old Maya had designed the memorial as a class assignment. She wanted to create a memorial that would touch people and help them draw their own conclusions about war.

It was 1981 when Maya was on her way home to Ohio for Thanksgiving vacation, she decided to stop in Washington, D.C., where the memorial was to be built. She stood on the ground between the Washington Monument and the Lincoln Memorial and looked at the surroundings. She wanted her work to be a part of the land, not overcome it. She envisioned the earth cut open and then healed. The wall of black granite would move between two worlds, one of the sun and one of darkness.

At school she sketched her idea in pastel crayons and then made a clay model of the monument. Part of the requirements stated that all the names of the killed and missing would be written on the memorial. She chose black granite because of its peaceful qualities. The angle of the monument would be purposefully directed toward the Washington Monument and the Lincoln Memorial. The concept was simple and direct.

But Maya Lin's design was not welcomed by everyone. Some thought that the design was too strong and not patriotic enough. Others thought that she was just too young to know what the Vietnam War was about. There were even claims of racism because the designer was Chinese American. Although over 650,000 people donated more than five million dollars for the project, construction was put on hold. The Vietnam Veterans Memorial Fund committee strongly defended the design. They understood that the memorial would tell the story of the men and women who died in the war. Finally, the committee was given permission to begin construction.

More than 150,000 people attended the dedication on Veterans Day in 1982. At the ceremony, the names on the wall were read, families and friends ran their fingers over the names of loved ones and the Vietnam Veterans were remembered.

Maya Lin relates the story of when she visited the memorial, "I searched out the name of a friend's father. I touched it and I cried. I was another visitor, and I was reacting to it as I had designed it."

13

GA1323

ACTIVITY
MONUMENTS

Monuments help us remember famous people or events in history. A monument may be as small as a plaque or as large as a mountain. Make a list of five monuments. They can be located in your hometown or anywhere in the nation.

	Name of Monument	**Who/What It Is Dedicated To**	**Location**
1.			
2.			
3.			
4.			
5.			

GA1323

Laurence Yep
Children's Author

Laurence Yep is an award-winning children's author who has captured the imagination of young people with such books as *Dragonwings*, *Child of the Owl*, *Sweetwater* and *Sea Glass*. His books are known for their historical accuracy and attention to detail.

Dragonwings was Laurence's first success. The book is based on a true story of a young Chinese American aviator who lived at the turn of the century. The novel won the Newbery Honor and the International Reading Association 1976 Children's Book Award. Laurence spent more than four years gathering historical information and writing the book.

Laurence was born in San Francisco in 1948 and raised in the nearby town of Fillmore. There his parents owned and operated a grocery store. As a boy he already enjoyed writing and conducting experiments in chemistry. By the age of 18 he had sold his first story to a science fiction magazine.

As he was growing up, Laurence realized that there were virtually no books about Chinese Americans like himself. He discovered information about his heritage through the stories his grandmother used to tell him. She told stories about his family and fairy tales from China. These stories served as an inspiration for many of his books. Laurence dedicated his book *Dragon of the Sea* to his grandmother and the sense of heritage she gave him.

These days Laurence spends most of his time in front of a word processor writing novels for children as well as for adults. Two of the titles of adult science fiction are *Shadowland* and *Monster Makers, Inc.* He has even designed a computer game called *Alice in Wonderland*. With his wonderful stories, Laurence Yep has enriched many lives. He describes his work this way, "I like to think I opened up a window to let people go into my imagination."

ACTIVITY

Laurence Yep
Children's Author

BE A SCIENCE FICTION WRITER

"When I was growing up
there were no books about Chinese Americans.
Science fiction talked about adapting to
other cultures, languages and environments."

Laurence Yep

What is the difference between science fiction and other forms of fiction? Science fiction creates new worlds based on probabilities that spring from the writer's imagination.

Write your own science fiction story. Create a world different from ours. Explore the possibilities of new life-forms and technologies. Be sure to give a detailed description of the setting and your characters.

For inspiration read *Sweetwater* by Laurence Yep or other science fiction like *Star Wars* or *A Wrinkle in Time* or other young adult books of that type.

Yoshika Uchida has written more than twenty-four books and short stories for children. Among them are Japanese folktales translated into English and several novels about the Japanese American internment experience. She credits her family for giving her a love of reading and writing, and pride for being Japanese American.

Melissa Macagba Ignacio was thirteen when she wrote *The Philippines: Roots of My Heritage*. Melissa's story describes how she discovered more about her cultural heritage by visiting the Philippines in 1976.

Ruthanne Lum McCunn writes books for both children and adults. Her most popular children's books are *Pie Biter* and *Sole Survivor*. Born in San Francisco, she has lived in many parts of the world including Hong Kong and Great Britain.

ACTIVITY
Asian-Pacific Americans
CHILDREN'S AUTHORS

Make a list of your favorite stories. Begin with those stories you enjoyed as a very small child. Explain why you liked each story.

Katherine Cheung
Pioneer Pilot

The year was 1932. Spectators gathered to watch the Los Angeles Air Show. A biplane dipped and turned. The pilot skillfully maneuvered the flying machine into a routine of breathtaking aerial acrobatics. When the plane landed, out stepped Katherine Cheung, the first Chinese American woman to earn a pilot's license in the United States.

Katherine was a music student at the University of Southern California. Her parents weren't sure if they wanted their daughter to be taking chances in the sky above them. So Katherine decided to take them on a flight. Her parents were so impressed by Katherine's flying ability that they enthusiastically encouraged her to continue.

During the early 1930's, pilots did not have sophisticated navigational equipment. Katherine fondly remembers one cross-country race from Los Angeles to Cleveland, Ohio. She navigated across the treacherous peaks of the Rocky Mountains with only a compass in hand. On her way back, the compass failed. Undaunted, she kept flying until she found a small clearing and made a smooth landing in Calexico, California.

Katherine belonged to an organization of women pilots known as the '99 Club. The club president was the famous flyer, Amelia Earhart. The club members held races and performed in air shows together.

Katherine was fascinated by flying, even when she was still a teenager living in China. But at that time Chinese women were not allowed to fly. It was not until she came to the United States was she able to take flying lessons. As she soared through the skies, she realized just how much she would like to share her experience and establish a women's flying school in China.

In order to raise money for the flying school, she flew across the United States, giving speeches and organizing air shows. With the first $7000, she placed an order for the first of several planes she hoped to buy, but on the day it was to be delivered, Katherine was told it had crashed. She felt that she had let her contributors down. With her hopes of opening the school dashed, she never flew again.

Katherine Cheung was a pioneer in the field of aviation, a skillful pilot and a faithful member of the '99 Club. She will be remembered for her contributions to flying and, most of all, her desire to help others.

GA1323

ACTIVITY
Katherine Cheung
Pioneer Pilot

CROSS-COUNTRY AIR RACE

On the map below, plan a cross-country air race.

The rules are

- You must stop in at least six cities.
- Draw in the cities and name them.
- Mark your start and finish.

19

GA1323

ACTIVITY
Katherine Cheung
Pioneer Pilot

THE HISTORY OF AVIATION

Go to the library and look for the section on aviation. Find a book on one of the following subjects:

- The history of flight
- Women in aviation
- Modern commercial aircraft
- The future of aviation
- The Wright Brothers

Write a paragraph about one of these subjects from the book (or books) you select.

AIRCRAFT DESIGN

Design an airplane of the future. Include all the features for the following:

- Safety
- Speed
- Comfort
- Good looks

Include a logo (symbol) for your own airline.

YOU ARE THE PILOT

Write one page of what it would be like if your were a pilot with your own plane and if you could take your family for a ride. How do you think they would react? Where do you think members of your family might like to go?

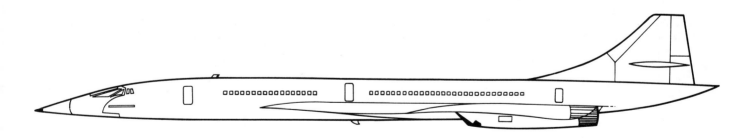

GA1323

How Man Wong

An American Explorer in China

How Man Wong has been described as a "Space Age Marco Polo." A modern day explorer, he uses both state-of-the-art technology and traditional methods to discover more about the world we live in. Born in Hong Kong, he is now a resident of Southern California. He works as an explorer, journalist and photographer for *National Geographic* magazine.

Since 1982, How Man has led over six expeditions throughout the far provinces of China. In his travels he learned that over fifty-five ethnic minorities live there. He also found that each group has its own unique traditions, food, clothing, language and religion.

During his 1986 trip to China, How Man made a great discovery while exploring the mighty Yangtze River. China's longest river, the Yangtze, spans more than 4000 miles from the source

high in the Tibetan Plateau to the mouth which empties into the East China Sea. How Man and his expedition team flew in more than two tons of specialized equipment and supplies. Yet, even four-wheel drive vehicles, inflatable boats and research instruments modified for high altitudes were no match for rough mountain trails, mud slides and freezing temperatures. At 20,000 feet above sea level, modern technology was traded for three helpful yaks. Yaks are a type of mountain buffalo used by the Tibetan nomads for farming and transportation. Using the yaks as pack animals, the expedition was able to forge the cold glacial waters of the river with relative ease. After nearly a year of exploration, the team reached the official source of the river. But further inquiry and research by How Man led him to believe that the true source lay further to the east. How Man's research and tenacity proved to be worthwhile when his team discovered the source of China's longest river several miles east of the "official" site.

How Man Wong has explored and photographed many parts of the world, including Central and South America. He is president of the China Exploration and Research Society. He is an adventurer whose inquisitive spirit guides him to challenge the great frontiers of our globe.

21

GA1323

ACTIVITY
How Man Wong
An American Explorer in China
EXPLORING THE WORLD

Take an expedition to the uncharted corners of the world. Where would you go? Who would be a part of your expedition team? Plan your trip from food to special equipment.

- Locate where you would like to go and draw a map.

- Make a list of the people you would like to be a part of your expedition team. Write down each job next to the team member's name.

- How will you get there? Describe your transportation.

- Make a list of equipment that you will take along.

- List your date of departure and your expected return.

GA1323

Events in Asian-Pacific American History
Filipino Americans

1587   Filipino sailors land in present day California with the Spanish explorer Pedro de Unamuno

1898   Under the Treaty of Paris ending the Spanish American War, the Philippines becomes a protectorate of the United States. American influences in culture, education and language begin.

1903   Pensionado Act permits Filipino students to receive an education in the U.S.

1907   Legislative restrictions, such as the Gentlemen's Agreement and later the Immigration Act of 1924, halt the flow of Japanese laborers to America and create jobs to be filled by Filipino laborers.

1920   Filipino and Japanese plantation workers join together to end discriminatory practices in the workplace.

1927   The Filipino Federation of Labor is founded. The organization is created to protect migrant farm workers from unfair labor practices.

1929   The Depression creates greater competition for jobs everywhere. Violence and discrimination against Filipinos sharply rises.

1931   Filipinos who served in the United States military become eligible for citizenship.

1935   The United States declares the Philippines to be a commonwealth. Filipinos everywhere celebrate this first step toward national independence.

1946   The Philippines gain independence from Japanese occupation during World War II. The United States offers citizenship to all Filipinos.

Carlos Bulosan publishes his book, *America Is in the Heart.* It records the experiences of a young Filipino man living and working in the United States during the 1930's.

1965   Between 1965-1974 Filipino immigrants are the second largest group to enter the United States. They come from all walks of life. Many are professionals and technical workers.

1980   The U.S. census lists 775,000 people of Philippine ancestry living in the United States. The U.S. census projects that by 1990 Filipinos will make up the single largest Asian group.

GA1323

Eleanor Academia Magda

Musicologist

Follow your heart's desire, but when you make a decision, be sure that you are committed to doing it well.

Eleanor Academia Magda carries those words in her heart. They were given to her by her father who knew that she had something meaningful to give the world. Eleanor is a musicologist who studies Kulintang. Kulintang is the Philippine gong music that originated in the third century A.D.

Eleanor was born in Honolulu, Hawaii. She is of Filipino, Spanish, Chinese and Malaysian descent. Music was and still is part of her family's everyday life. She remembers hiding behind the piano when her sister was taking lessons. After she and everyone else had left, Eleanor would come out of hiding and repeat the music her sister had just learned, note for note. This remarkable feat was even more amazing when one discovers that she was only three years old.

A few years later her family moved to California, and Eleanor went on to learn new instruments and types of music ranging from classical to rock and rhythm and blues. She even played in dance bands with relatives and friends.

In 1980 she received a music scholarship from the University of Southern California. There she met a fellow musicologist who asked her the pointed question, "How can you call yourself a true musician if you don't know the music of your ancestors?" She took this question as a challenge and began to study Kulintang, the soul of her past.

Today Eleanor Academia Magda is the co-founder and executive program director of The World Kulintang Institute in Reseda, California. The institute's aim is to perpetuate the music and educate audiences about Kulintang and Filipino culture. Besides her work with the institute, Eleanor wrote, produced and played on two record albums, *Jungle Waves* and *Global Conversations*. She views her work not only as a means of preserving a piece of culture but as a bridge from the old to the new.

ACTIVITY
Eleanor Academia Magda
Musicologist

MUSIC OF THE WORLD

Find out what part of the world your ancestors are from. Go to the library and look up the following, and write a paragraph about each question.

- What kind of music is native to that part of the world?
- Are there any special musical instruments in that area?
- What sort of composers or well-known musicians come from there?

What is your favorite instrument? Go to the library and find out more about that instrument. Write a paragraph about each question.

- What sort of instrument is it (wind, percussion, etc.)?
- Where did the instrument originate?
- Name three famous musicians who play or played that instrument.
- Name a musical group that uses that instrument.

25

GA1323

Asian-Pacific American Women in Government

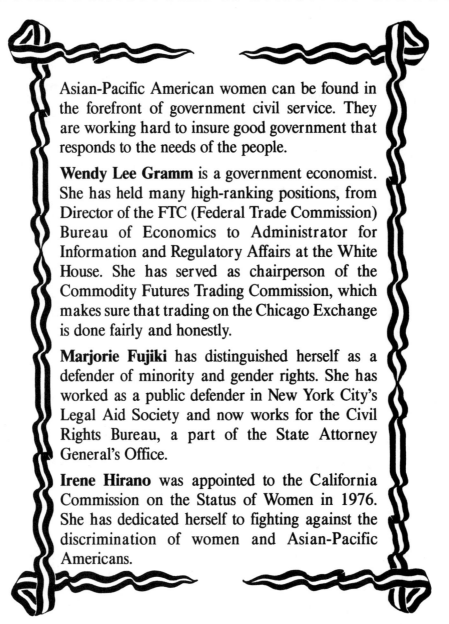

Asian-Pacific American women can be found in the forefront of government civil service. They are working hard to insure good government that responds to the needs of the people.

Wendy Lee Gramm is a government economist. She has held many high-ranking positions, from Director of the FTC (Federal Trade Commission) Bureau of Economics to Administrator for Information and Regulatory Affairs at the White House. She has served as chairperson of the Commodity Futures Trading Commission, which makes sure that trading on the Chicago Exchange is done fairly and honestly.

Marjorie Fujiki has distinguished herself as a defender of minority and gender rights. She has worked as a public defender in New York City's Legal Aid Society and now works for the Civil Rights Bureau, a part of the State Attorney General's Office.

Irene Hirano was appointed to the California Commission on the Status of Women in 1976. She has dedicated herself to fighting against the discrimination of women and Asian-Pacific Americans.

Write your answers to the following questions:

1. What is a government?

_____

_____

2. What are the responsibilities of a government?

_____

_____

3. What are the qualities that a government leader should have and why?

_____

_____

Share your answers with the rest of your classmates.

GA1323

Irene Natividad

Political Leader

If there is anything I'd like to be said about me, it would be that no matter how difficult, for a short time, I made a difference.

Irene Natividad is one of the nation's most effective political leaders. She is a strong advocate for women and Asian-Pacific Americans. She has her hand on the pulse of American politics and is often consulted on issues regarding presidential campaigns, child care and the environment.

Irene is active in several organizations. She is chairperson of the National Women's Political Caucus which consists of more than 77,000 members. This group assists women in winning elections and appointments to political offices. Since 1985 Irene was elected twice to be chairperson of that organization.

Irene Natividad is a Filipino American. She is committed to her ethnic background and urges others to do the same. Speaking to groups like the Asian-Pacific American Journalists, schools, and colleges, she urges people to take an activist role. She was honored by the Asian-Pacific Ameri-can Legal Defense and Education Fund for her many contributions to the community.

Irene recalls that she began her political career in 1968 while still a college student. She says she simply kept getting involved in different organizations and went from handing out leaflets for a presidential campaign to becoming one of the most regarded consultants in the Bush-Dukakis presidential race. She is particularly knowledgeable about the issues for women voters in election campaigns.

She has a busy schedule, usually the first in the office and the last to leave. Besides her knowledge about voters, she is very effective as a fund-raiser and someone who gives excellent press interviews.

She lives with her husband and son in Washington, D.C. Irene Natividad has made a difference. Her work has influenced organizations across America and helped Asian-Pacific Americans and women to gain a stronger voice in electoral politics on the local, state and federal levels.

27

ACTIVITY
Irene Natividad
Political Leader
FAMOUS WOMEN LEADERS

"If there is anything I'd like
to be said about me,
it would be that no matter how difficult,
for a short time, I made a difference."

Irene Natividad

Write a paragraph about a famous woman leader who made a difference in history. Include facts and general information about her life and accomplishments.

The following names represent just a few women leaders you may wish to write about:

- Queen Cleopatra of Egypt
- Joan of Arc from France
- Queen Elizabeth I of England
- Katherine the Great, Empress of Russia
- Queen Ka-Ahu-Manu of Hawaii
- Prime Minister Golda Meir of Israel
- Prime Minister Indira Gandhi of India

- Margaret Thatcher, former Prime Minister of Great Britain
- President Corazon Aquino of the Philippines
- Prime Minister Benazir Bhutto of Pakistan
- Winnie Mandela, Activist, South Africa
- Violeta Chomoro, President of Nicaragua

Queen Nefertiti of Egypt

Asian-Pacific American Judges

Defenders of Justice

Judge Herbert Choy became the first Asian-Pacific American to be appointed to a federal judgeship in 1971. He was named to the position by then President Richard M. Nixon. Judge Choy held that post until 1984 when he became a senior judge. Today he is retired but remains active in the legal community.

Irene Takahashi was appointed to the position of municipal court judge for Contra Costa County in 1988. After graduating from law school she served as deputy district attorney as well as a federal prosecutor before accepting her 1988 appointment from Governor Deukmejian.

Thomas Tang was appointed to the federal bench by President Jimmy Carter in 1977. He was the first American of Chinese descent to serve on the intermediate appellate court and the third Asian-Pacific American lawyer in the state of Arizona.

Ernest Hiroshige served as a Los Angeles district attorney for nine years before being elected to the South Bay Municipal Court in 1980. At age 36 he was appointed to the Superior Court. Ernest is a founding member of the Japanese American Bar Association and a founding member of the group Leadership for Asian-Pacifics. This organization is committed to furthering the leadership skills of Asian-Pacific Americans.

These are just a few members of the Asian-Pacific American legal community whose job it is to defend the American way of justice for all.

GA1323

ACTIVITY
The Law
WORD SCRAMBLE

1. wal _____ judge
2. laib _____ jury
3. iajl _____ justice
4. laelg _____ courthouse
5. yruj _____ lawyer
6. corder _____ federal
7. yerlaw _____ municipal
8. swtnies _____ sentence
9. eugjd _____ defender
10. deferal _____ legal
11. ejcusti _____ prosecutor
12. fendreed _____ jail
13. tencsene _____ witness
14. rotcuprose _____ record
15. niciumlap _____ law
16. tuorc seouh _____ bail

teh   fo   jutisce   cepae

Unscramble the words and place them in the correct order to form a common phrase.

30

Mel Red Recana

Judge

Mel Red Recana was the first Filipino American to become a judge on the United States mainland. He was born in 1939 in the town of Guinobatan in the Philippine province of Albay. His family was very poor, and it was not unusual for him to walk as far as ten miles on foot to attend school. Later he managed to go to college, worked as a court recorder and went to law school in the capital city of Manila.

In 1968, at the urging of his brother Jaime, a Fulbright scholar, Mel decided to move to the United States. At first he was not able to practice law, but after attending many trials in the Los Angeles courts and studying the different procedures, he felt he was ready to take the necessary bar examination. He passed the difficult test and became a lawyer. He worked for three years before being offered the job of Deputy District Attorney for Los Angeles. This was a great honor, but not as great as the one he received a few years later. It was on June 13, Filipino Independence Day. A large number from the Filipino community had gathered at McArthur Park to celebrate with music, folk dancing, activity booths and many other festivities. More than 10,000 people in all had gathered there for that special day. It was made even more festive when Mr. Recana was sworn in by Governor Jerry Brown to be the first Filipino judge on the U.S. mainland.

Today Judge Recana works as a municipal court judge in Los Angeles and teaches law at Pacific Coast University. He is married and has two sons who attend college.

Judge Recana speaks fondly of his father, who was the only policeman in the whole town of Guinobatan. "The only policeman in the whole town," Mr. Recana points out with a smile. Even though he had managed to get no more than a third grade education, he was a very intelligent man who continuously reminded his sons that education is the greatest gift anyone can receive. "It can't be stolen and you can't lose it," he would remind his boys, and neither Mel nor his brother Jaime ever forgot it.

Today, when children come to his courtroom on a field trip, he recalls the day when he walked so far to school, sometimes hungry, but always eager to learn. He likes to encourage children to follow their dreams, to educate themselves and to choose careers they will enjoy.

GA1323

ACTIVITY
Mel Red Recana
Judge
YOU BE THE JUDGE

Solve the following problem and write out your answer:

In a school yard two children are fighting over the same toy. Both claim that it is theirs. What sort of questions would you ask to find out who is telling the truth? What kind of solution or judgement would you prescribe?

_____

_____

_____

_____

_____

_____

_____

_____

_____

_____

_____

_____

Think of a problem you or any of your friends may have had recently. Write it out, and give it to the person on your right to solve.

_____

_____

_____

_____

_____

_____

_____

_____

_____

_____

GA1323

Asian-Pacific Americans in Education

Leaders in Education

These are just a few of the many talented leaders in the field of education. As in other professions, Asian-Pacific Americans hold positions in a variety of education specialties. They are teachers and teachers' aides, administrators, professors, deans and college presidents.

Dr. Paul Sakamoto was superintendent of the Mountain View-Los Altos Union High School District for fifteen years. He has been honored with many professional awards such as the Outstanding Young Educator Award from the Jaycees and the Distinguished Alumni Award from Michigan State University. He is also a consulting professor of education at Stanford.

Lily Sung has dedicated her life to education. Born in San Francisco in 1899, she has been honored by the Asian-Pacific American community for her work as an educator and an advocate for peace and the future of humanity. She says, ". . .honor, dignity and justice should be for all. I think education brings that about."

Yasuko Ishida Ito is a nisei activist for education. She has received such outstanding awards as the Woman of the Year Award from the City of San Mateo and the PTA Honorary Life Membership Award. She also spearheaded the JACL Community History Project which developed a program on the history of Japanese Americans in San Mateo County.

Chang-Lin Tien is the first Asian to head a major United States university. He is a chancellor at the University of California at Berkeley. In 1962 he was the youngest person ever to receive the Distinguished University Teaching Award. He is also internationally recognized for his knowledge in the area of heat transfer technologies.

Ronald Takaki is a Graduate Advisor of the Ethnic Studies Ph.D. Program. He has received numerous awards, including the Goldwin Smith University Lectureship at Cornell University and Berkeley's Distinguished Teaching Award. His Pulitzer prizewinning book, *Strangers from a Different Shore*, is a history of the Asian-Pacific American experience.

GA1323

ACTIVITY
Asian-Pacific Americans in Education
MEMORABLE TEACHERS

Do you remember a favorite teacher that you once had? Write what you liked about this teacher. What did you learn from him or her?

Helen Brown

Educator

Nearly 100 years ago, with the help of the U.S. Navy, the Philippine people overturned more than 350 years of Spanish colonial rule. At the time, Philippine and American leaders agreed that the country would win its independence as soon as the Spaniards turned over the capital city of Manila. But years passed and the American government did not keep its promise. While the flag and language changed, colonial rule continued. To strengthen the U.S. position, hundreds of American teachers were sent to the island country. Because the first ones arrived on the steamer *U.S.S. Thomas*, they promptly earned the nickname "Thomasites." Their mission was to teach the English language and American values to the local population and thus help unify the Philippine system of communications.

Helen Brown's father was a Thomasite and her mother the daughter of a provincial governor. She grew up in a large family as one of seven children and enjoyed a very comfortable life-style. At sixteen she was sent to the United States to become a student at the University of California at Los Angeles.

She recalls that she was always proud to be Filipino, even when people looked at her strangely and asked questions like, "How come you speak English so well?" "What kind of house did you live in?" or "Where are the Philippines?" Sometimes she grew frustrated and lonely because there was no one else from her country she could turn to. But, unexpectedly, support and recognition came from some of her teachers. It was this encouragement from teachers and friends, and of course her own determination, that led her to become the first Filipina graduate at UCLA.

In the 1960's she became one of the founders of ACT (Asians Coming Together), a group that addressed the social problems of Asian-Pacific Americans. ACT members learned to deal with problems ranging from learning disabilities to drug abuse. The group flourished, growing to ACT 2 and 3.

Throughout her career as an educator and advocate for the Asian-Pacific American Community, Helen Brown made it a point to teach people about Filipino Americans. She went out of her way to collect books, posters and other materials on the subject and even produced a slide show entitled *The Filipino and American in Me.*

In the 1980's she, her husband and four sons organized the Pilipino-American Library. Now retired from teaching, she remains active as commissioner of the Asian-Pacific American Education Commission for Los Angeles City Unified School District, oversees the library and lectures on the Filipino-American experience.

Helen Brown remains true to the Filipino and American part within herself and energetically goes on to tell others about the richness of her heritage.

GA1323

ACTIVITY
Helen Brown
Educator
EDUCATE YOURSELF

When Helen Brown came to the United States early in this century, she was asked many questions about her background. By using an encyclopedia, books and magazines about the Philippines, find out if you can answer the questions posed to Helen.

1. Where are the Philippines? Name at least one of the bodies of water around the Philippines. Name three neighboring countries.

2. Why do so many Filipinos speak English? Name another language spoken in the Philippines.

3. What is the capital city of the Philippines?

4. What sort of houses do Filipinos live in? Are the houses modern, similar to ours? Are some of them different?

5. What sort of articles are the newspapers printing about the Philippines (natural disasters, political events, etc.)?

_____

WRITE A LETTER TO HELEN BROWN

If you would like to find out more about the Philippines or Filipino Americans, write to Helen Brown at the *Pilipino-American Reading Room and Library in Los Angeles.

Pilipino-American Reading Room and Library
301 North Union Avenue
Los Angeles, California 90026

*The terms *Filipino* and *Pilipino* are both correct.

Events in Asian-Pacific American History

Japanese Americans

1639 Japan forbids emigration to the West. This self-imposed restriction will last for over two centuries.

1843 Japanese and Filipino plantation laborers join together to end racial discrimination in the pay scales.

1885 Japanese emigration begins to Hawaii and the U.S. mainland. By 1924, 200,000 will have immigrated to Hawaii and 180,000 to the mainland.

1919 Issei farmers own over 450,000 acres of land in California alone. Through their knowledge and skill in farming, they produce more than 10 percent of California's truck crops. Legislation such as the Alien Land Law of 1930 will try to prevent Asians from becoming successful landowners and from competing with established non-Asian farmers.

1930 The Japanese American Citizens League (JACL) is founded. The JACL is a nationwide civic and civil rights organization that represents the Japanese American community.

1942 In the midst of World War II, Executive Order 9066 mandates that all persons of Japanese ancestry be removed from designated areas in the west and placed into internment camps.

1952 The McCarran-Walter Act makes issei (first generation) Japanese Americans eligible for citizenship.

1980 President Jimmy Carter establishes the Commission of Wartime Relocation and Internment of Japanese Americans.

The U.S. census shows that 701,000 people of Japanese ancestry are living in the United States.

1988 President Ronald Reagan signs a law insuring redress and reparations to those Japanese Americans interned during World War II.

1990 The oldest Japanese Americans who had been interned receive reparations.

GA1323

Ellison Onizuka
Astronaut

Some people wish upon stars, while others reach for them.

Ellison Onizuka was someone who aspired to reach for the stars and became a space explorer. As a "sansei" or third generation Japanese American, he was not only the first Asian-Pacific American space shuttle astronaut, but also a man dedicated to his family, community and country.

Ellison was born on June 24, 1946, in Kona, Hawaii. His parents were grocery store owners who never expected that their small son who had trouble learning to ride a bicycle would someday travel in space. His favorite subjects in school were math and science. Ellison was an active leader and member of the Boy Scouts and 4-H. He earned the rank of Eagle Scout by working on money-raising projects for the Kona hospital, organizing a litter cleanup at a local park and more. Ellison was admired for his thoughtfulness towards others and his common sense. These childhood experiences would help to prepare him for his future career.

After high school, Ellison moved to the U.S. mainland and became an Air Force flight test engineer. He then married his wife Lorna and began raising a family. The couple had two daughters named Janelle and Darien.

In 1977 Ellison was selected to be a NASA space shuttle astronaut. His training involved long hours of learning about the equipment on the space shuttle, working under zero gravity conditions and taking classes in computer science and astronomy. Yet, even with his busy schedule, he always made time for his family and community activities.

Ellison's first space flight came in 1985 on the shuttle *Discovery*. Part of the crew's mission was to conduct health research on normal and diseased red blood cells in a weightless environment. Another experiment was to study the transfer of fluids between spacecraft still in orbit.

Three days and forty-eight orbits later, the *Discovery* landed at Cape Canaveral, Florida. Ellison enjoyed sharing the thrill of spaceflight with people. He often described the view of earth as "breathtaking."

On January 28, 1986, Ellison Onizuka was one of the seven crew members who tragically died when the space shuttle *Challenger* exploded on takeoff. Family, friends and the nation mourned the loss of these courageous Americans.

From your vantage point, your education and imagination will carry you to places which we won't believe possible. Make your life count—and the world will be a better place because you've tried.

Ellison Onizuka gave this message to the 1980 graduating class of Konawena High School. He believed in these words and proved them true.

GA1323

ACTIVITY
GET INVOLVED!

Ellison Onizuka was the first Asian-Pacific American in manned spaceflight. He was an active community member who always tried to do his best. His determination to do well for his family and community can be seen in his work aboard the space shuttle high above the earth.

Think about a project that you could do to help the people in your family, school or neighborhood.

Describe your project in the space below. Be sure to include the following information:

- What you plan to do
- How your project will help others
- What materials you will need
- When you plan to start and finish this project

  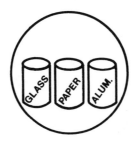 

GA1323

"Sox" Kitashima
Civil Rights Activist

"I'm outspoken. I don't hold anything back," says seventy-two-year-old "Sox" Kitashima. "Sox," whose real first name is Tsuyako, is a civil rights activist. Her organization, the National Coalition for Redress and Reparations or NCRR, has spoken out for the more than 100,000 Japanese Americans who as U.S. citizens were denied their constitutional rights and sent to internment camps during World War II.

In 1979 "Sox" testified before the commission holding hearings on Japanese American relocation and internment. She was one of the first to openly share her experiences in the internment camps. Many Japanese Americans were reluctant to step forward and talk about what happened, but "Sox" felt that this important part of history should not be ignored or forgotten.

Gathering her courage, she spoke to the commission about the way she and her family were forced to leave their home and friends with only a suitcase in each hand. She carefully described how her family of five had to live in a racetrack horse stall until they were moved to the drafty barracks of an internment camp in Utah. Yet most of all, she remembered the humiliation of seeing signs that read, "Japs not welcome here."

From 1979-89, the NCRR, the Japanese American Citizens League, and other groups struggled to pass a bill into law that would recognize the injustice of the Japanese American relocation and internment. "Sox" lobbied in Congress, collected petitions and forwarded over 25,000 letters to Washington, D.C., in hopes of getting the bill passed. After three tries, the redress and reparations bill was passed in August of 1988.

"Sox" Kitashima has worked with other civil rights defenders to give a voice to justice. She knows that the redress and reparations law will not erase the events of the past but will hopefully prevent a similar incident from happening in the future.

ACTIVITY
"Sox" Kitashima
Civil Rights Activist
OUR AMERICAN HERITAGE

The United States of America is the homeland to many different types of people. The diversity within our country is what makes it unique from other countries. Finding out about your heritage can help you understand yourself better. It can also help you appreciate other ethnic, cultural and religious backgrounds. After all, what makes our country special is that people from every part of the world live here together.

What is your ethnic heritage? Are you:

- Native American (American Indian)
- African American
- Asian-Pacific American
- European American
- Latino (from Central or South America)

- Arabic (Middle East)
- Persian (Iran)
- East Indian or Pakistani
- A combination of several backgrounds
- Other (not listed above)

Ask your parents, grandparents or other relatives where your family is from. List specific countries and family names if you can.

- Mother _____
- Father _____
Other family names: _____

- Country (s) _____
- Country (s) _____

Take a poll of three friends to find out what their heritages are.

- Name: _____ Heritage: _____
- Name: _____ Heritage: _____
- Name: _____ Heritage: _____

When someone says, "I'm an American," what does that mean? Being an American is more than just living in this country. It means understanding our heritage as individuals and as a group.

GA1323

ACTIVITY
"Sox" Kitashima
Civil Rights Activist
SPEAKING YOUR MIND

How do you feel about the environment, pollution, crime? How do you feel about your school, some of your fellow students or staying up late at home? Think about an issue that is very important to you. Write down that issue and an argument defending it. Present that issue and your argument in front of your class. Ask your classmates if they have opposing views, and let them argue those views. Afterward write down how your classmates' views, for or against yours, influenced you. Did your view remain the same or change?

1. Issue (problem):

2. Argument for or against that issue (include ways to solve problems):

3. Opposing views:

4. Resolution:

GA1323

Daniel K. Inouye
Senator

In 1959, Daniel K. Inouye became the first Japanese American to be elected to the United States Congress. Representing the state of Hawaii for more than thirty years now, Senator Inouye has gained prominence as a strong and just lawmaker and staunch defender of the United States Constitution.

Daniel K. Inouye was born in Honolulu, Hawaii, in 1924. His grandparents and father had come there from Japan to find work as laborers on the sugar plantations. As the oldest of four children, Daniel earned his first spending money by running errands for neighbors, cutting hair and baby-sitting. The Inouyes believed that it was important for their children to know about both their Japanese and American traditions, and like many of his friends, Daniel went to an American public school and a Japanese language school. As he grew older he developed an interest in the medical field and worked as a volunteer at a first aid station on the island of Oahu. He hoped that one day he would become a surgeon.

When Daniel turned eighteen, the United States found itself in the midst of World War II. To prove his loyalty to America, Daniel enlisted in the army. He was assigned to the 442nd Regiment made up of all Japanese Americans and led by mostly Caucasian officers. When the regiment was sent to fight in Italy, Lieutenant Inouye was wounded just two weeks before the war's end. His arm had to be amputated and with it went his aspirations of becoming a surgeon. But he did not lose heart. He turned to the study of law and believed that by entering politics he could fight against some of the injustices he saw.

Since then Senator Inouye has fought injustice in many forms. He has served on many important committees and was recognized for his work on the Watergate and Iran/Contra hearings. He has also led the way to insure fair and equal treatment for Asian-Pacific Americans and other minorities in the workplace and in schools. He is a member of the 442 Veterans Club and the Disabled American Veterans of Hawaii.

Senator Inouye has spent more than thirty years of his life defending our now 200-year-old Constitution, first as a soldier and then as a legislator. To him the Constitution is not just a piece of paper with words on it, but a guide that guarantees equal protection under the law to Americans who have lived here for generations as well as those immigrants who have just arrived.

GA1323

ACTIVITY
Daniel K. Inouye
Senator
QUIZ

True or False:

T F 1. Daniel K. Inouye was the twelfth Asian-Pacific American to be elected to Congress.

T F 2. He grew up in Wyoming.

T F 3. He earned pocket money by cutting hair, baby-sitting and running errands.

T F 4. When he was young he hoped to become a lawyer.

T F 5. He has gained national and international recognition by serving on the agriculture sub-committee.

T F 6. Daniel K. Inouye is a senator representing the state of Hawaii.

Fill In:

Daniel K. Inouye's parents and grandparents came from the country of _____. They came to Hawaii to find work on the local _____. Daniel is a _____ generation Asian-Pacific American. In World War II, Lieutenant Inouye fought in the country of _____ _____. Today he is well respected for his knowledge of, and defending, this famous American document: _____

GA1323

Japanese Americans
The Decision to Fight

For many Japanese Americans it was a hard decision, whether or not to fight in World War II. The United States was not only at war with Germany and Italy but also with Japan. This meant that Japanese Americans faced the possibility of doing battle against their own kinsmen.

Questioning their loyalty, the U.S. government interned most Japanese Americans after the outbreak of hostilities in 1941. But soon it became clear that all manpower, including that of Americans of Japanese descent, would be needed to win the war.

Early in 1942 the U.S. War Department decided to form the 100th Battalion made up of nearly 1500 Japanese Americans from Hawaii. Later the 442nd Regiment was assembled on the U.S. mainland. Many members, both volunteers and draftees, came from the internment camps where they and their families had been sent earlier. Still doubtful of their loyalty and leadership abilities, both units were commanded mostly by Caucasian officers.

First the 100th Battalion was sent to Italy where the men fought courageously. Tragically, they also suffered many casualities. They were joined by the 442nd Regiment, and together they fought many battles from Italy to France and Germany. At one battle they were ordered to rescue a battalion of soldiers from Texas who had been surrounded by German troops. In days of bitter fighting, half of the Japanese Americans were killed or wounded to rescue the 275 men of the "Lost Battalion."

"Go for Broke" was the motto of the 100th Battalion and 442nd Regimental Combat Team, and they proved the words with deeds of remarkable heroism which cost many their lives.

The final irony came when members of the regiment broke through one of the gates at the infamous Dachau Concentration Camp. As they liberated the inmates in early 1945, many of their own family members were still behind barbed wire in the United States.

The Japanese American 100th Battalion and 442nd Regiment became the most decorated outfits of World War II: ten presidential unit citations, 3915 individual medals, among them the Medal of Honor. Over 700 men lost their lives and thousands were wounded. They proved their loyalty to America.

GA1323

ACTIVITY
Japanese Americans
The Decision to Fight
WAR

Briefly answer the following:

1. What do you know about war?

2. What is your personal opinion about war?

3. How would you feel if you were told to fight against the people from the same country where you, your parents or grandparents are from?

4. What do you think about the choice that Japanese Americans of the 100th Battalion and 442nd Regimental Combat Team made to fight in the U.S. Army (while their families were interned in camps)?

Fred Takahiro Hattori
Poet

Takahiro Hattori was born in Nagoya City, Japan, on October 19, 1906. When he was 18 his father sent for him and his mother to help in the senbei (rice cookie) factory he had established in Los Angeles. Takahiro, who adopted the American name Fred, was the last member of his family allowed to immigrate into the United States, because in 1924 Congress passed a law barring Asians from coming to live in the United States.

Fred Hattori still remembers coming off the ship in San Pedro harbor, the 1932 Olympic Games in Los Angeles and the devastating 1933 earthquake in Long Beach. He also remembers the hard times of the Depression when his father had to close the factory. While the economic picture looked bleak, Fred turned more and more to the poetry his father and grandfather had taught him. It is called tannka and is the oldest form of Japanese poetry. More than one thousand years ago, before it was written down, people passed it on by word of mouth from generation to generation. The typical tannka has thirty-one syllables broken into five lines. The following is an example with a loose translation:

5 syllables	SHIKISHIMA NO	What is the spirit
7 syllables	YAMATO GOKORO O	Of Japan
5 syllables	HITO TOWABA	Someone asked
7 syllables	ASAHINI NIOU	Facing the morning sun
7 syllables	YAMA SAKURA BANA	It is the mountain cherry blossom.

Fred thought up many poems like these while working in the family flower business. Typically the themes deal with nature, life and feelings.

Why does he write?

"Because with poetry I am never alone. It always makes me think."

In 1937 he found a teacher in Shasui Takayanagi, the foremost tannka poet in the United States. During World War II, while interned at Heart Mountain, he became a teacher himself, starting with a small group that grew to more than one hundred. He also edited and published the monthly poetry review "Rocky Tannka Kai." After the war Fred worked as a gardener, continued to teach poetry and published two books on tannka, each holding more than three thousand poems of his students' work.

His work is not only respected in the United States (his books are in the Library of Congress) but also in Canada, Mexico and Japan. Japanese readers consider "Gendai (modern) Tannka" which uses English and other foreign words as a complement to the classical Japanese form.

GA1323

ACTIVITY
Fred Takahiro Hattori
Poet
TRADITION

Describe two or more traditions in your family. What sorts of things have been passed on to you by a family member? For example, skills in woodworking, sewing, cooking or playing of musical instruments, songs or stories about your family, nursery rhymes and so on.

1. Name two activities or traditions:

    a.

    b.

2. Who taught this to you?

3. How old were you when you learned a. and b.?

4. Do you think you are a better person for knowing this?

5. Do you intend to pass this knowledge on to another family member?

GA1323

Events in Asian-Pacific American History
Korean Americans

1885   A small number of Korean students and political refugees emigrate to the United States.

1903   Koreans begin to emigrate to the United States and Hawaii to escape Japanese rule in Korea and to seek work.

1908   Hankuk Puin Hoe, the first Korean women's organization, is founded in San Francisco. The group promotes Korean language education and ethnic solidarity.

1951   From the end of the Korean War to 1964 a second group of immigrants arrive. This group is made up of wives of American servicemen, war orphans and students.

1952   The McCarran-Walter Act allows for Korean-born immigrants to become eligible for citizenship.

1965   The Immigration and Naturalization Act of 1965 initiates the third and most current wave of immigrants from Korea.

1980   The U.S. census shows 354,000 persons of Korean ancestry living in America.

Byron Kim

Artist

Byron Kim is an artist. He works with many different types of materials, including oil paint and latex rubber. He describes his work as "tactile," which means it may be touched. This is unlike most art, which may only be looked at. Byron likes to do his work in a way that shows the steps he took to complete it. He is fascinated with the science of art, how things work and the properties of different materials.

Sometimes Byron will get an idea for a method or a project when he least expects it. He remembers one summer when he was exhausted from working, he picked up a ballpoint pen and started doodling. After a while, he really liked what he saw and decided to use the doodles as a part of his technique.

Byron studied medicine in order to become a doctor, like both of his parents, but then realized that he really wanted to be an artist. Both of his parents were very supportive of his change in career. He says his parents are proud of their Korean heritage. They lead by example, not just with words.

Byron believes that "art represents all of us," and that includes representation from all groups in America. Byron works at the Skowhegan School of Painting and Sculpture in Maine. He has shown his artwork at the Bronx Museum and at PSI Gallery in Queens, New York.

Byron Kim is an emerging artist who values the process of art as much as the product.

GA1323

ACTIVITY
Byron Kim
Artist
PROCESS ART

Have you ever worked on an art project where you didn't know how it would turn out, where you just had fun with different materials?

Set up an art project in which you can experiment with several different materials. Use your imagination and think about the process of doing something without worrying about the end product. Work as long as you wish. You determine when you are done. Be bold! You only have to please yourself, no one else.

Here are a few suggestions for materials and what can be done with them. This is just to get your ideas started. It would be better if you used just your own.

Materials		Method	Tools
paper	cork	draw	pencil
wood	aluminum (cans)	paint	brush
leaves	wax	tear	scissors
sand	nails	cut	spoon
glue	plastics	scrape	hammer
paint	plants	drip	saw
cloth	feathers	bend	sandpaper
string		knot	hand drill

For inspiration look up artists like Man Ray, Braque, Picasso and others who used discarded objects to create their art. Some artists, particularly those of the Dada movement, were more interested in the process of making something than the final product. Some even built art that would self-destruct.

GA1323

The Arts

When speaking of art, it is usually divided into the visual arts and the performing arts. Visual arts include painting, sculpture and crafts. Among the performing arts are usually music, dance and theater. Of course there is a lot of overlap between the two, especially motion pictures, television and performance art. For example, MTV with its music, dance and animation packs both visual and performance art into a neat video format.

Asian-Pacfic Americans are active in all the arts, traditional and modern, in the United States and internationally. Often, when Asians and art are mentioned together, people like to think of the traditional arts like koto (zither) and taiko (drum) music or the hula dance. It is true that some Asian-Pacific Americans are most interested in traditional music, dance and painting. For example, there are more than fifty Filipino folk groups in the United States alone. But there are also artists like those of the Asian American Dance Collective of Los Angeles who combine the old with daring new experiments. Another artist who likes to mix the old and new is Masami Teraoka. His modern messages like *McDonald's Invades Japan* are painted in the exquisite style of an eighteenth century Japanese master.

Like most artists, Asian-Pacific Americans work in very personal ways as well as in the mainstream. There are many Asians in American films and television. Do you know these world-class artists?

- Isamu Noguchi, sculptor
- Seiji Osawa, conductor
- Yo Yo Ma, cellist
- David Hwang, playwright
- Amy Tan, novelist
- Jeanne Nakano, dancer
- Mira Nair, documentary filmmaker

There are many more. To name them all and describe their work would take many pages. It is worth remembering though that Asian-Pacific Americans have left their mark and are still giving much to the arts.

GA1323

ACTIVITY
Asian-Pacific Americans in the Arts
POINTS FOR THE ARTS

How many disciplines within the arts can you name? Make a list and collect one point for each answer. Mark each answer with a V (visual art), P (performing art) or B (both) and earn another point.

The Arts

How many artists can you name? Make a list and collect three points for each answer. For each Asian-Pacific American artist, collect five points.

Dr. Sammy Lee
Diver

A sports official once told Sammy Lee that no person of color would ever become a national diving champion. Sammy proved him wrong by not only winning the national championship in 1942, but by going on to become one of the nation's greatest divers.

Sammy Lee studied medicine at the University of Southern California and then joined the United States Army Medical Corps in 1942. He earned a place on the U.S. Olympic Team in 1948. At the London Olympics, Sammy won a gold medal for diving. In the 1952 Olympics held in Helsinki, Sammy won another gold medal. He was the first Asian-Pacific American to win two gold medals in Olympic diving competition.

In 1956 Lee was selected by President Dwight D. Eisenhower as a presidential representative to the Olympic Games in Melbourne. In 1958 he became the first Asian-Pacific American to win the James E. Sullivan Award for being an out-standing American sportsman. A member of the President's Council on Physical Fitness, Sammy was the diving coach of Greg Louganis for several years. Today, Sammy is a physician living in Southern California.

Sammy Lee fought unfair treatment and discrimination with his talents and perseverance.

ACTIVITY
Dr. Sammy Lee
Diver
PHYSICAL FITNESS

How fit do you think you are on a scale of one to ten? Mark your answer.

not very fit   **very fit**

1   2   3   4   5   6   7   8   9   10

How much physical exercise do you get each day? Mark your answer.

½ hour   1 hour   2 hours   3 hours   more

What kind of exercise (activity) do you do? Write it down. (For example, walking to school, playing ball in the school yard, physical education, building a tree house, sports, etc.)

1. _____

2. _____

3. _____

Do you think you need more physical exercise? Yes _____ No _____

What do you think you could do more of? _____

_____

What about nutrition?

What do you eat for breakfast? _____

What do you eat for lunch? _____

What do you eat for dinner? _____

How many soft drinks do you consume per day? _____

How many sweets do you eat per day? _____

Do you regularly eat cereal, lettuce, vegetables, whole grain bread? Yes _____ No _____

How do you think you could improve your diet? _____

_____

GA1323

The Fight Against Disease

Progress toward eliminating and reducing major illnesses due to heart disease, cancer and AIDS is being made by the best and brightest in the medical profession. Among them are Asian-Pacific Americans who are making a difference in the battle against life-threatening disease.

Yuet Wai Kan, M.D., is a professor of medicine at the University of San Francisco. He is responsible for identifying the cause of thalassemia. Thalassemia is an inherited blood disease common among Asians. His research has helped in the diagnosis of the disease. For his work, he was elected to the National Academy of Science in 1986. He is now working on a cure for thalassemia.

Mimi C. You, Ph.D., is a cancer epidemiologist who discovered the cause of nasopharynx cancer. Nasopharynx cancer occurs in the nasal cavities. Gathering information on the diet of the patients, she discovered that the disease was caused by a certain type of preserved fish they ate.

Garrett Lee is a pioneer researcher responsible for a special laser device that clears the arteries of patients undergoing heart surgery. The laser enters clogged arteries and vaporizes the fatty deposits that can lead to heart attacks.

Flossie Y. Wong-Staal, Ph.D., is a medical researcher fighting to overcome Acquired Immune Deficiency Syndrome or AIDS. With her colleagues at the National Cancer Institute in Bethesda, Maryland, she conducted research that was vital to the discovery and diagnosis of the disease.

GA1323

ACTIVITIES
The Fight Against Disease
MEDICAL FACTS

Below are nine statements. Circle all of those that are correct.

1. Thalassemia is a form of heart disease.

2. Sammy Lee discovered the cause of nasopharynx cancer.

3. Flossie Y. Wong-Staal is fighting the battle against AIDS.

4. Yuet Wai Kan is a cancer epidemiologist.

5. Garrett Lee's laser vaporizes fatty deposits in clogged arteries.

6. Nasopharynx cancer occurs in the nasal cavities.

7. Mimi C. You discovered thalassemia.

8. The National Cancer Institute is in Bethesda, Maryland.

9. Thalassemia is an inherited disease common among Asians.

MEDICAL CODE

Using the code below, fill in the blanks to discover the words in the word bank.

1. _ _ _ _ _ _ _ _

2. _ _ _ _ _ _

3. _ _ _ _ _ _ _ _

4. _ _ _ _ _ _ _

5. _ _ _ _ _ _ _ _

WORD BANK
doctor, illness, medicine, patient, research

Events in Asian-Pacific American History

Southeast Asian-Pacific Americans

1954 France, with United States aid, loses war against Vietnamese Communists. Vietnam is split into two countries.

1964-75 United States commits to fight in Vietnam.

1975 Over 130,000 Vietnamese (including ethnic Chinese), 70,000 Laotians, 10,000 Mien and 60,000 Hmong seek refuge in the United States. The number of refugees sharply increases over the next two decades.

 Southeast Asian families learn to adjust to a new way of life. American sponsors help families settle into communities. Tensions arise as cultural and racial conflicts occur. Families work to take part in American culture while still preserving their own rich cultural heritage.

1979 In Cambodia (Kampuchea), the Pol Pot regime is overthrown by Vietnam. More than 100,000 Cambodians find refuge in the United States.

 Studies on Southeast Asian immigration note an increase in employment for refugees. Though many are professionals from a variety of fields, they often have to accept jobs below their skill levels.

1984 The *San Jose Mercury News* reports that 350,000 of the 696,000 immigrants from Southeast Asia live in California.

GA1323

Boy Scout Troop 100

Hmong Americans

In 1981 a group of two hundred Hmong students arrived at Edison High School in Minneapolis. The Hmong were mountain tribesmen who became refugees in their own country, Laos. They had gone through war, refugee camps and traveled thousands of miles to start a new life in the United States. The high school students were required to take bilingual education in their own language and English and began to participate in school activities.

One of the teachers, Mr. Dave Moore, was asked if he could hold a Boy Scout meeting for the new students. He agreed and started the meeting by serving refreshments and teaching the Pledge of Allegiance. Later they played some games and got to know one another. The word got out, and soon other Hmong students began to join. They held meetings once a week and started to go on outings and camping trips. This was the beginning of the Minneapolis Troop 100.

Dave Moore, the troop leader says, "This group never just hangs around saying they're bored. They always have something to do, even if it is making a whistle out of a dandelion stem." These young men don't take anything for granted. After going through extreme hardship, they value the opportunities available in this country.

One Scout named Yee Chang taught the Hmong language to members of the Minneapolis community. Another Scout, Dao Bay Ly, set up an employment agency for high school students. Pao Ly Vu wrote a collection of children's stories that chronicled their journey from Laos to America. A number of those first Hmong Scouts attained the rank of Eagle Scout and went on to college.

Today, of the eighty Scouts in the troop, seventy-eight are Hmong. There are now first and second-generation members in the troop. Being Scouts was a great way for them to make friends, learn English, find out more about our country and prepare for American citizenship.

GA1323

ACTIVITY
Boy Scout Troop 100
Hmong Americans
I'M BORED!

List ten activities you could do when you get bored, excluding television watching and napping.

Find out more about Hmong Americans. Look up the article about them in the December 1988 issue of *National Geographic* magazine. Ask the reference librarian if there are any other articles about the Hmong, and look up at least one of them.

GA1323

Dustin Nguyen
Actor

The year was 1975. Saigon, the capital of South Vietnam, was in the midst of war. Nguyen Xuan Tri was twelve years old when his family fled Vietnam aboard an American cargo ship. Nguyen Xuan Tri is known today as Dustin Nguyen (pronounced "when"). He played officer Aoki on the television series *21 Jump Street*. Dustin is one of the few Asian-Pacific Americans to have regularly appeared in a television series.

When Dustin's family arrived in the United States in 1975, they were sent to a refugee camp in Arkansas. The family encountered many hardships while trying to settle in their new country. The language was unfamiliar to them and all of their belongings were either lost or stolen. The comfortable life that they led in Saigon was only a memory.

Dustin's family was sponsored by a church group in Missouri. They became one of the first Vietnamese families to live in the state. At the beginning, there were some tense moments among Dustin's classmates until everyone got to know one another. Children were mean and made fun of him. Dustin was afraid of making mistakes in speaking English. He channeled his energy and talents into sports, acting and the martial art Tae Kwon Do.

After graduating from high school, Dustin enrolled in an acting school located in California. Instead of taking money from his parents for his education, he waited on tables at a coffee shop. Dustin wanted to be independent.

His first acting jobs were small parts on soap operas and shows like *Magnum P.I.* Acting became a way of expressing himself. He developed a confident attitude. He believed in his acting ability and knew that he would be successful even if it took him twenty years to reach his goal.

He didn't have to wait long before he became a regular on *21 Jump Street*.

Dustin Nguyen is a role model for young adults seeking to become actors. He has worked to portray positive and accurate images of Asian-Pacific Americans in his role on television.

GA1323

ACTIVITY
Dustin Nguyen
Actor
WHAT'S YOUR NAME?

When Nguyen Xuan Tri came to the United States he changed his name to Dustin Nguyen. In Vietnam the first name given is the family name and the last name is what we call the first name or given name. In other words, Tri is his first name and Nguyen his family name.

Often when immigrants come to this country, they may assume a new, and for us, simpler name that may be easier for Americans to pronounce and remember. In the past immigration officials would often give immigrants a new name, shorten it or spell it incorrectly which then remained on their records. Also, immigrants had the option to assume new names when they arrived.

What do you know about your name? Ask your family members if they know where and how your name originated, and if it has a special meaning.

1. Your family name:_____

2. In what part of the world (country) did it originate? _____

3. Does it have a special meaning? _____

How did you get your first (given) name? Ask your parents why they picked it and what it means.

1. Your first (given) name: _____

2. Why did your parents pick it? _____

3. What does it mean? _____

   GA1323

The Image of Asian-Pacific Americans in Motion Pictures and Television

Asian-Pacific Americans have been in motion pictures and television for more than sixty years. In the early days, they were mainly portrayed as cartoon-like figures, speaking broken English and performing menial tasks. To make matters worse, these parts were often played by non-Asians who taped their eyelids and were told to "act like Asians." As a result, Asians and Asian-Pacific Americans were judged by these stereotypes. Films and television programs did not show them as they were in real life. Instead, Hollywood created an image of Asians as caricatures. The same was true for other ethnic groups such as Native Americans, African Americans, Italian Americans and Mexican Americans.

Today, the entertainment industry has become more sensitive to these ethnic stereotypes. Groups like the East West Players of Los Angeles and the Association of Asian-Pacific Artists give a collective voice to Asian-Pacific Americans in the arts. One purpose of these groups is to educate people about the negative effects of these stereotypes and to insure that Asian-Pacific Americans have access to a range of acting roles. Actors like Mako in *The Wash,* John Lone in *The Last Emperor of China* and Frances Nyuen on the TV show *St. Elsewhere* are shining examples of nonstereotypic roles for Asian-Pacific Americans.

Mako is a thirty-year veteran of stage, film and television and is a founding member of the East West Players theater group. In 1966 he was nominated for an Oscar as best supporting actor. His performance in the film *The Wash* is a strong and realistic portrayal of an aging Japanese American man facing serious family problems.

Frances Nyuen was born in France to a Cambodian father and a French mother. She came to Hollywood in 1956 and played the shy Liat in the movie *South Pacific.* Three decades later, she played the self-assured Dr. Paulette Kiem on the TV series *St. Elsewhere.*

Pat Morita was the first Asian-Pacific American to have his own prime time television series. The famous actor has held leading roles in *The Karate Kid* films and in the 1987 TV series *Ohara.*

Rosalind Chao played many realistic portrayals of Asian-Pacific American characters in her career. Among her roles was that of a Korean war bride in the 1984 series *After M*A*S*H.*

George Takei was the helmsman Mr. Sulu in the *Star Trek* television and film series. He created a character who has been popular with "Trekkie" fans since the 1960's.

GA1323

ACTIVITY
Images of Asian-Pacific Americans
MEDIA STEREOTYPES

Describe a stereotype of an ethnic group you saw on television (including commercials or movies).

1. What was the character's ethnicity (Arab, German, Mexican, Russian, etc.)?

2. How was this person portrayed?

3. Did the person have an accent?

4. Was the accent exaggerated or made to sound funny?

5. Was the person portrayed as not being intelligent?

6. Was the person portrayed as being mean or deceitful?

7. What do you know that is positive about this ethnic group?

Discuss your answers with your teacher.

Events in Asian-Pacific American History
Asian Indians*

1907   Workers from India arrive in America. Famine and an agricultural system imposed by the British colonial government force many Asian Indians to seek work in other countries. Many are sons of small landowners who are sent to the United States to help financially support their families in India.

1914   Padma Chandra becomes the first Indian woman to become a student at the University of California at Berkeley.

1916   Kanta Gupta becomes the first Indian woman to apply for United States citizenship.

1920   Asian Indians negotiate for better wages in the American work force. They have become sharecroppers and farm owners.

1946   Asian immigration reopens. Anti-Asian legislation also affects the Asian Indians by reducing the population living in the United States to less than two thousand.

1947   The nations of India and Pakistan are created.

1951   Dalip S. Saund of California is the first Asian-Pacific American to be elected to Congress.

1965   The Immigration Act increases the number of South Asian immigrants entering the United States.

1970   Professionals from large cities in Pakistan immigrate to the U.S. Many settle in the Northeast.

1971   East Pakistan becomes the nation of Bangladesh.

1980   The U.S. census notes 525,000 persons of Asian Indian descent living in America.

* The term *Asian Indians* includes among others Pakistanis, Bangladeshis and Sri Lankans.

Asian-Pacific American Novelists

Younghill Kang was one of the first Asian-Pacific American writers. At the turn of the century, Younghill left his native Korea to live in the United States. The story of his journey is told in the novels *The Grass Roof* (1931) and *East Goes West* (1937). Younghill's books are a document of one Korean immigrant's search for a home in a new country.

Carlos Bulosan was a contemporary of Younghill Kang. In the 1930's he became one of the most celebrated writers in the United States. His short stories and novels describe the struggle of the Filipino laborer during the time of the Great Depression. A self-educated man, Carlos Bulosan gave a voice to the Filipino American community that is still being heard today.

One of the most widely read authors on American college campuses today is **Maxine Hong Kingston**. Her novels *Warrior Woman* and *Tripmaster Monkey* blend Chinese myth and magic together with contemporary Chinese American life. Raised in Stockton, California, Maxine grew up in a home where storytelling and writing were valued family traditions.

Amy Tan's parents thought that someday she would become a neurosurgeon. Instead she became a best-selling writer. *The Joy Luck Club* is Amy's first novel. The story is about four first-generation Chinese mothers and their "Americanized" second-generation daughters. Having grown up in Oakland, California, Amy visited China for the very first time in 1987. There she discovered a meaningful part of her heritage in meeting her Chinese relatives.

GA1323

ACTIVITY

Asian-Pacific American Novelists
DID THIS REALLY HAPPEN?

Many writers like Carlos Bulosan and Amy Tan draw upon their own experiences to create a novel or short story. Write a story based on a true event that happened in your life. Give the story a new twist by adding something different that really did not happen. Read the story to your classmates, and see if they can tell what event really happened and what did not happen.

Amy Tan

Bharati Mukherjee
Novelist

Bharati Mukherjee sees America as a land that offers hope and independence. It is a place where people are given the chance to prove themselves based on their accomplishments and abilities, a place to dream and make dreams come true.

Growing up in Calcutta, India, Bharati lived a very predictable life. Everything was prescribed for her. Her traditional society determined who she could play with, where she could go and even the man she would eventually marry. Bharati wanted something different. She discovered this when she was eight years old and traveled with her parents to England and Switzerland. She remembers her feelings of excitement as she explored the new countries and cultures.

In the early 1960's Bharati went to college in the United States. There she met her husband, a Canadian, Mark Blaise. After college, the couple moved to Montreal, Canada, and Bharati estab-

lished herself as a prominent writer. The racism that she encountered there prompted her to write her 1981 essay "An Invisible Woman." By speaking out and writing about the problem, Bharati shocked many people who did not believe that racism existed in Canada. Nearly a decade later, her efforts to raise the consciousness of people are now being recognized.

Today, Bharati is a novelist and a professor at the University of California at Berkeley. Her short stories and novels center on the experiences of South Asian immigrants, their arrival to a new country and their challenges to succeed. Bharati Mukherjee realizes the many risks she had to take to leave her safe and secure life in India. She sees the new immigrants as having the same courage and energy as those who first arrived.

Here (America), I'm not afraid to be impassioned. I'm not afraid to make mistakes.

ACTIVITY
Bharati Mukherjee
Novelist
RACISM

Bharati Mukherjee spoke out against racism. Define *racism* in your own words.

_____

_____

_____

_____

Give an example of racism drawn from American history. Describe the event and whether or not anything was done to correct it.

_____

_____

_____

_____

What are your feelings about this event, and what was done about it?

_____

_____

_____

_____

GA1323

Subrahmanyan Chandrasekhar

Nobel Prizewinning Astrophysicist

In 1983 Subrahmanyan Chandrasekhar was awarded the Nobel Prize for physics. An astrophysicist, Chandra (as he is called by his friends) studied the planetary structure of white dwarves and laid the groundwork for the discovery of black holes in space. He earned many honors, including the National Science Medal and the Gold Medal of the Royal Astronomical Society.

Chandra was born in Lahore, India, on October 19, 1910, into a distinguished family of scientists and scholars. Chandra was especially interested in the work of an uncle who was a Nobel prizewinning physicist. Inspired by his uncle's work and that of other physicists, Chandra decided to be a scientist at an early age. At 18 he published his first research paper in the *India Journal of Physics.*

In 1930 he left India for Great Britain. There he continued to study physics and became fasci-nated with the theory of collapsing stars, otherwise known as "white dwarves." He began to analyze current studies and found a flaw in established theories on the subject. According to Chandra, not all stars eventually collapse and become white dwarves. Chandra's calculations were not only accurate, they led to the discovery of invisible neutron stars and black holes in space.

In 1937 Chandra emigrated to the United States. He accepted a position as a research associate at the University of Chicago. Today he is retired and resides with his wife Lalitha in the Chicago area.

Subrahmanyan Chandrasekhar was not award-ed the Nobel Prize until years after his discoveries. Many scientists did not believe that his calcu-lations were correct. Chandra believed in himself and in the accuracy of his reasoning. When his theory was proven to be correct, he was recognized as a scientist truly ahead of his time.

GA1323

ACTIVITY
Subrahmanyan Chandrasekhar
Nobel Prizewinning Astrophysicist
THE NOBEL PRIZE

Look up the following information in your encyclopedia, journals or books:

1. Subrahmanyan Chandrasekhar won the Nobel Prize for Physics. Look up the name of another winner and fill in the blanks below.

Name: _____

From which country: _____

Year received: _____

Award received for: _____

2. List three facts about his or her work.

   a. _____

   _____

   _____

   b. _____

   _____

   _____

   c. _____

   _____

   _____

GA1323

Asian-Pacific Americans in Farming

Since the days when they came to work on the sugar plantations of Hawaii, more than 100 years ago, Asian-Pacific Americans have been a major force in the development of American agriculture. Working the land as laborers and sharecroppers, the first Asian-Pacific Americans turned deserts and swamplands into rich, fertile fields. They saved their money and began to buy land to farm on their own.

By the early 1900's, they produced nearly 85 percent of all fruits and vegetables grown in California. Jealous of their success and wanting the land for themselves, many non-Asian farmers enacted laws to limit what the Asian-Pacific Americans could do. The Alien Land Law of 1913, for example, prohibited the sale of land to Asians. Then came laws that halted Asian immigration in 1934 and Executive Order 9066 which caused most Japanese Americans to lose their land. In spite of these restrictions, Asian-Pacific Americans kept going, and by the 1950's, many were involved in agriculture once more.

Today the participation of Asian-Pacific Americans in farming has greatly broadened to include farm owners, produce shippers, greengrocers, soil conservationists, horticulturists and many more. They are active in their communities, land management and the politics of agriculture, not only for themselves but for all those who rely on America's abundant crops.

Sam Sakamoto has been a farmer and horticulturist for over forty-five years. He has served as a member of the state and federal soil conservation board of directors for over eighteen years. He is also responsible for starting a local chapter of the FFA (Future Farmers of America) for a high school in Santa Cruz, California.

Kim Hyung-Soon and **Kim Ho** created the Kim Brothers Company in 1913. The business involved everything from fruit wholesaling to the operating of large orchards, nurseries and packing facilities. Their company also developed new varieties of peaches and nectarines.

Carlos Bulosan, the famous Filipino American writer, was the son of a farmer. On his arrival to America, one of the many jobs he held was farm laborer. Following the crops, from picking apples in Washington to peas in California, he tried to help his fellow laborers by organizing unions and later writing about the Filipino American experience in the 1930's and 1940's.

Clifford Low is a soil chemist who owns and operates Perry Laboratories in Watsonville, California. His job is to help farmers diagnose problems with soil, and then find ways to increase productivity.

GA1323

ACTIVITY
Asian-Pacific Americans in Agriculture
FARMING WORD SEARCH

```
T I T V F O L F A E L H A F B P
S O R E U F A R M A E O A E S L
E E A G R I C U L T U R E R E A
V R N E R E O I I Z M T V T S N
R C S T O L N T E I A I R I U T
A A P A W D S Z N L V C R L O S
H F O B S E U G W I R U O I H O
N L R L E C M P I O T L T Z N U
I O T E L U E E P S H T C E E W
A W F S I D R S L O G U A R E A
R E E R N O I T A G I R R I R T
G R O C E R Z S N U L E T B G E
T S K C A P E R D W E A T H E R
```

Find the following words in the puzzle:

tractor	fertilizer	consumer
agriculture	crops	weather
horticulture	fruit	pests
farming	vegetables	light
irrigation	soil	furrows
produce	land	transport
greenhouses	grocer	harvest
flowers	plant	acre
grain	water	pack
field		

GA1323

Harry Singh

Heartland Farmer

The Singh family farm has been operating in Oceanside, California, for nearly half a century. Today the farm is a nationwide business that yields over 900 acres of produce.

Its founder, Harry Singh, was born Hossiar Singh in Noormahl, India, during the early 1900's. At the age of sixteen, he came to the United States with plans to attend college. Soon after arriving, Harry's father died and his family was unable to pay for his college expenses. Harry decided to stay in the U.S. and began working as an accountant to farmers in Colorado and Arizona. Harry then moved to New Mexico where he met and married his wife Oclides.

Harry and Oclides were partners in everything they did. In 1941 they decided to move to Oceanside, California, where they leased a few acres of land from the government to farm tomatoes and celery. The first few years were especially hard. Eighteen-hour days were common

for the young couple trying to start a new business and a family. The Singhs built their own work sheds, constructed packing crates by hand and personally delivered their produce to the shipping companies.

Saving their money, they were able to start purchasing the land they had leased. Harry wisely invested his money in his farm, and it grew. He became a prominent community member and established himself as an active participant in local and federal politics. In fact, he became known for his keen sense of judgement and was sought out by Presidents for his political views.

Harry Singh died in 1982. Oclides, their two sons, and three daughters continue to operate the company in Oceanside. Harry's contributions to the farming industry and his sense of civic duty are a legacy the Singh family still continues in his memory.

GA1323

ACTIVITIES
Asian-Pacific Americans in Farming
FARMING

List as many jobs as you can think of that are related to agriculture. You may work alone or with a partner. Think of all the jobs that are required from growing a seedling to bringing the food to your store or supermarket.

_____

_____

_____

_____

_____

_____

_____

_____

Imagine what it would be like if there were no agricultural production in the United States. How would you get your food? Describe in three or four sentences what you think it would be like.

_____

_____

_____

_____

_____

_____

_____

_____

_____

_____

_____

_____

_____

GA1323

Events in Asian-Pacific American History

Pacific Islanders

1778   Approximately 300,000 native Hawaiians live in the Hawaiian Islands. The population is decimated to 35,000 by 1890. Opening trade with the West brings a disruption of the existing culture and unknown diseases such as cholera and smallpox.

1848   The Great Mahele of 1848 permits the purchase of Hawaiian land by private owners. Western enterprises in sugar, pineapple and other areas begin to take over.

    The demand for large masses of cheap labor leads to the immigration of virtually all Asian groups and from many European countries as well. Though sometimes pitted against each other, these groups of immigrants often work together in the fields and band together to improve labor conditions.

1893   Queen Liliuokalani tries to gain independence for the Hawaiian Islands. She is overthrown in a coup assisted by the U.S. Navy.

1899   The United States acquires Samoa and utilizes it as a naval base until 1950. Today the U.S. still maintains sovereignty. Western intrusion forces the Samoans to change many of their traditions and customs.

1920   Filipinos, Japanese, Chinese, Spanish and Portuguese laborers join together to protest unfair working conditions in the sugarcane fields and mills.

1941   Japan attacks Pearl Harbor, Hawaii, on December 7, 1941. Among the many people of the islands who help defend Pearl Harbor before and after the attack are thousands of Japanese loyal to the United States.

1959   Hawaii gains statehood in the United States of America.

1970   A renewed interest in traditions, art and ethnic identity is kindled among young people of Hawaiian descent. The Council of Hawaiian Organizations meets to look at the educational and economic needs of native Hawaiians.

1980   The United States census notes a total of 259,566 Pacific Islanders living in the United States. This includes Polynesians, Micronesians and Melanesians. Hawaiians make up 85 percent of the Pacific Islander population.

GA1323

The Jets

A Tongan American Rock Group

What is it like to be a member of a Tongan American rock band made up of seven brothers and sisters? The Jets, otherwise known as Leroy, Eddie, Haini, Rudy, Kathi, Elizabeth and Mona Wolfgramm would be able to tell you. With such hits as "Rocket 2 U," "Crush on You" and "Make It Real," the group has made its mark on America's pop music scene.

Based in Minneapolis, Minnesota, The Jets have a fast-paced schedule of performances, recording sessions and promotional appearances to maintain. Their concerts are a mix of popular dance music, slow ballads and even a traditional Polynesian dance number. Each member of the group sings, dances and plays at least one musical instrument.

In 1988 The Jets completed an eighty-city tour across the United States. The band has also toured in Asia and Europe, with hopes of playing in Tonga. Going on tour is not always easy. They sometimes miss going to the movies with friends, school activities or just hanging out around the house. The band tours with either one or both parents and tutors to help with schoolwork. Concerns get expressed at weekly family meetings. While touring can sometimes be hard, the group realizes the many opportunities and benefits that go along with being a part of a popular band.

The Jets know that they are role models for young people. They believe that it is important to let everyone know what families can accomplish when they work together. They have also appeared in public service messages for the Just Say No Foundation, encouraging kids and teens to stay away from alcohol and drugs.

The Jets are proud of their Tongan American heritage. Leroy, the oldest of the group, was the only child born in Tonga, a Polynesian island located about two thousand miles south of Hawaii. The rest of the Wolfgramm's seventeen children were born in the United States. The family speaks both Tongan and English. They hold many of the traditional Tongan family values and customs. The Jets are not only a band, but a family that works together. As one of the few Asian-Pacific artists in the rock world, they continually strive to be successful as musicians and a family.

ACTIVITY
The Jets
A Tongan American Rock Group
FAMILY

Describe an event when your family worked together to accomplish something. What kind of activity was it? Who participated? Did you accomplish your goal? How did you feel?

_____
_____
_____
_____
_____
_____
_____
_____
_____
_____
_____
_____
_____
_____
_____
_____

GA1323

Auntie Mary Kovich
The Art of Lei Hulu

Through the ancient Hawaiian craft of lei hulu or "feathermaking," Auntie Mary Kovich teaches about the spirit of "Ka Ha-awai Me Ke Aloha," which means sharing with love and aloha. She is a respected member of the Polynesian American community for her efforts to preserve the rich traditions of Hawaiian culture.

Mary was born in Hawi, Hawaii, on June 3, 1915, of Portuguese and Hawaiian descent. The name Auntie, a term of respect, was given to her much later in life. Mary was raised by her father and two grandmothers. It was from her Hawaiian grandmother that she learned the art of lei hulu.

Lei hulu involves the stitching together of brightly colored feathers into capes, gowns, headpieces, leis and other festive apparel. Long ago these outfits were reserved for Hawaiian royalty, but today they are used for many different types of special occasions.

One of very few people who have the knowledge and are willing to pass it on, Auntie Mary is the founder and president of Lei Hulu, an organization that teaches feathermaking and its importance in Hawaiian culture. When she teaches, Mary tells her students that they must not charge money to teach others the lei hulu. To do so would bring bad luck. She says that the "Hawaiian way" has also become the motto of her organization. "Ka Ha-awai Me Ke Aloha," teaching people with love and aloha, has graduated many students who are Hawaiian or who are Hawaiian at heart.

Auntie Mary has been honored by the Polynesian community in many ways. She has received the Humanitarian Award, the Hawaiian of the Year Award given by the Hawaiian Intercouncil and has been recognized by the Hawaiian Daughters Guild for her fund-raising efforts to establish student scholarships and to help restore the Iolani Palace in Hawaii.

Auntie Mary not only respects her heritage but has spent a good part of her life preserving it. Through individual efforts like hers, the beauty of Hawaii and its culture will still be enjoyed by generations to come.

GA1323

ACTIVITY

Auntie Mary Kovich

RITUAL FEATHERS

Imagine a grand procession of Hawaiian royalty. They are wearing glorious feather capes, headpieces and staffs created through the ancient craft of lei hulu.

In the old days, Hawaiian royalty would appoint special people as bird catchers. These bird catchers would place a honey-like, sticky substance on the bark of a tree and with it catch birds. They would then select a few feathers from each captured bird and set it free. With this method, thousands of feathers could be collected without harm to the birds. The magnificently colored feathers were then fashioned into royal costumes like those for King Kamahameha. Long ago the feathers were tied together with coconut bark. Today, feathermakers like Mary Kovich use a needle and thread.

Think of another culture that uses feathers as part of their costume (today and long ago). Describe how the feathers are used. Describe what ceremonial function they serve (if any).

ACTIVITY
Auntie Mary Kovich
OUR 50th STATE, HAWAII

Go to your atlas and look up the Hawaiian islands. Label the following islands:

Hawaii	Molokai
Maui	Oahu
Kahoolawe	Kauai
Lanai	Niihau

Locate one of the following geographic features:

bay	lake
volcano	river
mountain	beach

Name the ocean surrounding Hawaii. _____

Name the capital city. _____

When did Hawaii become the fiftieth state? _____

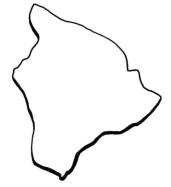

GA1323

Leo and Branscom Richmond

Actors

Leo and Branscom Richmond are father and son. Leo worked as an actor for many years, and Branscom is an actor and stuntman. Together their film and television careers span over fifty years.

It all started in the early 1920's when Leo was a boy growing up in Tahiti. While collecting tickets at Papa John Chaves' motion picture theater, he developed a deep and lasting interest in movies. For hours he would watch the silent screen and dream of being in a film himself one day. Ten years later, after moving to California, he got his chance. He landed some small parts that led to a role in the Bob Hope, Bing Crosby, Dorothy Lamour road show pictures. He also met his future wife in Hollywood who was originally from Hawaii. She bore their son Branscom in 1955.

Branscom started in show business when he was still very small. His father was helpful in getting him parts in movies like *Donovan's Reef* with John Wayne and *Mutiny on the Bounty* with Marlon Brando. Besides that his father gave him some good advice: "Remember these five things," he would say. "They are timing, chance, good fortune, persistence and talent. There will come a time when you must take a chance and choose. By choosing carefully you will make your own good fortune. You must be persistent and use your talents to keep that fortune."

Branscom believes that those words guided him to become the successful actor and stuntman he is today. He has performed in more than 100 movies and 250 television shows. He says he plays mostly bad guys, but his children Maro-uo, Fairai and Leiohu aren't afraid of him. To them he's just "Dad." His stunts have caused him to fall 55 feet, turn over in cars and walk through blazing infernos. But throughout, safety is his main concern. Each event has to be carefully planned and executed.

Children often ask Branscom how they can become stuntmen. He simply repeats his father's words with some encouragement of his own.

Branscom lives with his wife, a former Miss Hawaii, and their three children in Tarzana, California.

ACTIVITY
Leo and Branscom Richmond
Actors
THE PACIFIC ISLANDS

Among the many people who live in the Pacific Islands are

Polynesian: Hawaiian, Samoan, Tahitian, Tongan and Tokelauan

Micronesian: Guamanian, Saipanese, Tinian Islander, Mariana Islander, Marshallese and Palauan

Melanesian: Fiji, Papua New Guinean, Solomon Islander, New Hebrides Islander

Find out more about the Pacific Islands and the people who live there.

See how many islands you can locate on a globe or world map. By just using the globe or map, write down as many facts as you can about the islands you find.

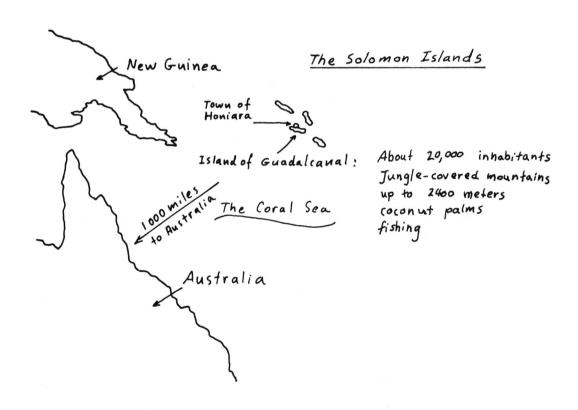

ADDITIONAL ACTIVITIES
Asian-Pacific Americans
HOLD A SEMINAR

Get together in groups of three or four. Select someone to take notes. Hold a discussion on one of the following topics related to Asian-Pacific Americans or think of your own topic.

- **The First Immigrants**

    What would it be like to leave the only country you know?

    Describe what it might be like to be an immigrant in the 1800's and an immigrant today.

    What problems might you encounter in a new country?

- **Famous Asian-Pacific Americans in Sports**

    Make a list of some of the Asian-Pacific Americans in amateur or professional sports.

    What does it take to be an athlete today?

- **Stereotypes About Asians and Asian-Pacific Americans**

    What is a stereotype?

    What are some of the stereotypes about Asians and Asian-Pacific Americans?

    Are stereotypes harmful? Why or why not?

    What can you do to avoid stereotypes?

After you have finished your discussion, be prepared to share what you've talked about with the rest of the class.

GA1323

ACTIVITY
Asian-Pacific Americans
CROSSWORD PUZZLE

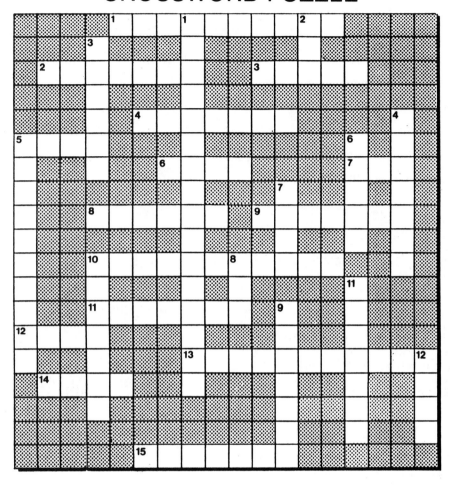

Across

1. Actor Dustin Nguyen is an American of _____ _____ descent.
2. The United States of _____
3. Hawaii became a _____ in 1959.
4. _____ is the record of past events.
5. George Takei played Mr. _____ in *Star Trek*.
6. The California _____ Rush of 1849 brought the first major group of Chinese to America.
7. Laurence Yep wrote *Child of the* _____
8. Katherine Cheung was the first Chinese American woman to earn a _____ license.
9. In 1988 President Ronald Reagan signed a bill to give Japanese American war internees _____ and reparations.
10. Connie Chung and Ken Kashiwahara are television news _____
11. The study of nature and the physical world is _____
12. Canton and Hong Kong are major _____ cities of China.
13. Almost all Asian-Pacific Americans have contributed to the field of _____
14. The abbreviation for the Japanese American Citizens League is _____
15. Asian-Pacific American athletes have won medals in many events of the _____ Games.

Down

1. The western section of the _____ Railroad was mainly completed by Chinese workers.
2. The _____ of Japan is the body of water between Japan and China.
3. The U.S. _____ is a record of the number of people who live in the United States.
4. Carlos _____ is the author of *America Is in the Heart*.
5. A _____ is a broad and often untrue generalization of a group of people.
6. The Asian country located south of China
7. The _____ are a Tongan American rock band.
8. To tell an untruth is to _____
9. The _____ Ocean borders most Asian countries and the American West Coast.
10. Judge Mel Red Recana's job is to insure that _____ is carried out.
11. Tai Babalonia, Kristi Yamaguchi and Tiffany Chin are all Asian-Pacific American _____
12. Vietnam is located _____ of the Philippines.

85

ACTIVITY
Asian-Pacific Americans
WHO IS THIS?

1. He is the first Asian-Pacific American to be elected to the United States Congress. _____

2. She helped to preserve the ancient gong music of the Philippines by founding The World Kulintang Institute. _____

3. He started a nationwide farming business in Oceanside, California. _____

4. She teaches the craft of lei hulu, or Hawaiian feathermaking. _____

5. He won the French Open tennis tournament in 1989. _____

6. He was the first Asian-Pacific American space shuttle astronaut. _____

7. He is a Hollywood stuntman whose father was also in acting. _____

8. He is an explorer who discovered the true source of the Yangtze River. _____

9. She is one of the nation's most effective political leaders and has been chairperson for the National Women's Political Caucus. _____

10. He was the first Filipino American to become a judge on the United States mainland. _____

11. He was a Nobel Prizewinning astrophysicist who studied the planetary structure of white dwarves and black holes in space. _____

12. She has been the anchor on the CBS nightly news and has hosted her own prime time television shows and specials. _____

Chung	**Inouye**	**Chandrasekhar**	**Chang**
Wong	**Singh**	**Richmond**	**Academia-Magda**
Kovich	**Recana**	**Natividad**	**Onizuka**

GA1323

Asian-Pacific Americans
BOOK REVIEW

Find out more about the Asian-Pacific American experience. Read a book about Asian-Pacific Americans and write a book review. Be sure to cover the following points in your review:

- Title of your book
- Author's name
- Brief description of the plot, characters and setting
- Your opinion about the story and the way it was written
- Were the Asian-Pacific Americans portrayed in a realistic or stereotypic way?

Here are some suggested readings that you might enjoy.

Sachie, a Daughter of Hawaii by Patsy Saiki (1977)

Park's Quest by Katherine Paterson (1988)

Ellison Onizuka: A Remembrance by The Onizuka Memorial Committee (1986)

Dark Sky, Dark Land: Stories of the Hmong Boy Scouts of Troop 100 by David L. Moore (1989)

The Philippines: Roots of My Heritage by Melissa Macagba Ignacio (1977)

Journey Home and *Journey to Topaz* by Yoshiko Uchida (1971, 1978)

Illustrated History of the Chinese in America by Ruthanne Lum McCunn (1979)

Dragonwings by Laurence Yep (1977)

Kim-Kimi by Irwin C. Hadley (1987)

Tales from Gold Mountain by Paul Yee (1989)

GA1323

Asian-Pacific Americans in Sports
SPORTS TIME LINE

1920's   **Duke Kahanamoku**
Surfer and Olympic diver

1924   **Charlie Pung**
Swimmer, Olympic 100m back-stroke

1940's   **Vicki Manolo Draves**
Diver, U.S. outdoor diving champion 2 years; Gold Medal, diving, 1948 Olympics

1942   **Dr. Sammy Lee**
Diver, National and Olympic champion

1943-45   **"Prince" Oana**
Henry Kauhane Oana
Baseball outfielder and pitcher for Detroit Tigers and Philadelphia Phillies

1950's   **George Taniguchi**
Jockey for 15 years

1964-65   **Masanori Murakami**
Baseball pitcher, San Francisco Giants

1970's-80's   **Tai Babalonia**
Figure skater, 5-time U.S. champion, 2-time Olympic team, 1979 World Champion

1970's-80's   **Peanut Louie Harper**
Tennis pro, 20-year career, 14 national junior titles, 10 Wimbledon tourneys

1972   **Jesse Kuhaulua**
Sumo wrestler, Emperor's Cup

1980   **Liane Sato**
Volleyball, 1980 MVP, Jr. Nationals

1981   **Ben Apuna**
Football linebacker, New York Giants

1984   **Tiffany Chin**
Figure skater, Olympic skater, World Jr. Champion

1985   **Kevin Asano**
Judo, '85 National Gold Medal

1982-88   **Insook Bhushan**
Table Tennis, National Women's Champion, 8-time member, U.S. team

1983-86   **Mayumi Pejo**
Tae Kwon Do, U.S. Olympic team

1980's   **Lenn Sakata**
Baseball infielder, New York Yankees

1980's   **Greg Louganis**
Diver, multiple Olympic Gold Medal winner

1980's-90's   **Kristi Yamaguchi**
Figure skater, National Gold Medal winner

1980's-90's   **Michael Chang**
Tennis pro, '89 French Open Champion

1986   **Brady and Bryant Sih**
Sailing, Double Youth Sail Champions

1987   **Sabrina Mar**
Gymnastics, Athlete of the Year

1987   **Jimmy Kim**
Tae Kwon Do, 3-time U.S. champion, 2-time International Champion

1989   **Junior Seau**
Football, San Diego Chargers

1989   **Jesse Sapolu**
Football, San Francisco Forty-Niners

1990   **Atlee Hammaker**
Baseball, San Francisco Giants

GA1323

ACTIVITY
Sammy Lee
OLYMPIC EVENTS

See how many Olympic events you can think of in ten minutes. Compare your answers with a friend. Make a master list with your whole class. Go to the library and check your answers.

1. _____
2. _____
3. _____
4. _____
5. _____
6. _____
7. _____
8. _____
9. _____
10. _____
11. _____
12. _____
13. _____
14. _____
15. _____
16. _____
17. _____
18. _____
19. _____
20. _____
21. _____
22. _____
23. _____
24. _____
25. _____
26. _____
27. _____
28. _____
29. _____
30. _____

For more information about the Olympic Games or your favorite sport, send your inquiries to:

The Amateur Athletic Foundation Library*
2141 West Adams Blvd.
Los Angeles, California
90018

*The Amateur Athletic Foundation Library was given to the city of Los Angeles by the Olympic Games of 1984.

GA1323

ACTIVITY
Asian-Pacific Americans
AMERICAN HISTORY POSTER

Make a giant classroom poster of American history with your classmates. Include significant events and contributions of all ethnic groups. Use illustrations, photographs or even real objects to create your poster. Use the "Events in Asian-Pacific American History" sheets and your local library to help you determine what events you will include.

GA1323

Selected Bibliography for Teachers

Endo, Takako, et al. *Japanese American Journey: The Story of a People.* San Mateo, CA: JACP., 1985. A collection of historical information, biographies and short stories to be used with students.

Kitano, Harry, and Roger Daniels. *Asian Americans: Emerging Minorities.* New Jersey: Prentice Hall, 1988. A teacher resource book that features Chinese, Japanese, Filipinos, Koreans, Asian Indians, Pacific Islanders and Southeast Asians and the current issues they face as Americans.

Ignacio, Melissa Macagba. *The Philippines: Roots of My Heritage.* San Jose, CA: Filipino Development Associates, Inc., 1977. A young Filipino American girl explores her heritage.

Moore, David L. *Dark Sky, Dark Land: Stories of the Hmong Boy Scouts of Troop 100.* Minnesota: Eden Prentice, 1989. The Boy Scouts of Troop 100 tell their story of transition from war torn Laos to a new life in the United States.

Ogawa, Dennis M., and Glen Grant. *Ellison Onizuka: A Remembrance.* Hawaii: The Onizuka Memorial Committee, 1986. The poignant biography of Ellison Onizuka, space shuttle astronaut.

Paterson, Katherine. *Park's Quest.* New York: E.P. Dutton, 1988. Katherine Paterson weaves a touching story with an Arthurian flair about a boy wanting to learn more about his father, who died in Vietnam.

Sing, Bill, editor. *Asian-Pacific Americans.* Los Angeles, CA: National Conference of Christians and Jews, Asian-American Journalists Association and Association of Asian-Pacific American Artists, 1989. An excellent resource on Asian-Pacific Americans. The handbook offers information on avoiding stereotypes, demographic statistics, a glossary of resources and much more.

Takaki, Ronald. *Strangers from a Different Shore: A History of Asian Americans.* Boston: Little, Brown and Company, 1989. The Pulitzer-nominated book chronicles the Asian-Pacific American experience.

Tan, Amy. *The Joy Luck Club,* New York: G.P. Putnam & Sons, 1989. A wonderful story of mothers and daughters for everyone to read.

Uchida, Yoshiko. *The Best Bad Thing.* New York: Atheneum, 1983. This award-winning novel about a Japanese American girl who discovers that sometimes there really is a silver lining in a dark cloud. Other books by Yoshiko Uchida are *Jar of Dreams, Journey to Topaz, Journey Home* and *The Happiest Ending.*

Yep, Laurence. *Dragonwings.* New York: Harper and Row Junior Books, 1977. One of Yep's first major works, *Dragonwings,* is the story of the Chinese American aviator, Fong Joe Guey. Other books by Laurence Yep are *Dragon of the Lost Sea, Child of the Owl, Sea Glass, Mountain Lights* and *The Rainbow People.*

For more information on Asian-Pacific American literature for students, contact:

JACP Inc.*
414 East Third Avenue/P.O. Box 367
San Mateo, California 94401

*Include $2.00 for catalog requests.

GA1323

Answer Key

page 44
1. F
2. F
3. T
4. F
5. F
6. T

Fill In: Japan, sugar plantations, second, Italy, the Constitution

page 57
The true statements are 3, 5, 6, 8 and 9.

1. research
2. doctor
3. medicine
4. patient
5. illness

page 73

T	I	T	V	F	O	L	F	A	E	L	H	A	F	B	P
S	O	R	E	U	F	A	R	M	A	E	O	A	E	S	L
E	E	A	G	R	I	C	U	L	T	U	R	E	R	E	A
V	R	N	E	R	E	O	I	I	Z	M	T	V	T	I	N
R	C	S	T	O	L	N	S	E	I	A	I	R	I	L	T
A	A	P	A	W	D	S	N	L	V	C	R	U	O	I	S
H	F	O	B	S	E	U	G	W	I	R	U	O	I	Z	O
N	L	R	L	E	C	M	P	I	O	T	L	T	Z	E	U
I	O	T	E	L	U	E	E	P	S	H	T	C	E	E	W
A	W	F	S	I	D	R	S	L	O	G	U	A	R	R	A
R	E	E	R	N	O	I	T	A	G	I	R	R	I	R	T
G	R	O	C	E	R	Z	S	N	U	L	E	T	B	G	E
T	S	K	C	A	P	E	R	D	W	E	A	T	H	E	R

page 86
1. Inouye
2. Academia-Magda
3. Singh
4. Kovich
5. Chang
6. Onizuka
7. Richmond
8. Wong
9. Natividad
10. Recana
11. Chandrasekhar
12. Chung

page 85

Crossword:
- 1 across: VIETNAMESE
- 2 across: AMERICA
- 3 across: STATE
- 4 across: HISTORY
- 5 across: SULU
- 6 across: GOLD
- 6 down / K: KOWL... (7 OWL)
- 8 across: PILOTS
- 9 across: REDRESS
- 10 across: JOURNALISTS
- 11 across: SCIENCE
- 12 across: PORT
- 13 across: AGRICULTURE
- 14 across: JACL
- 15 across: OLYMPIC
- 1 down: TRN...
- 3 down: CONSTITUTION
- 4 down: BULOSAN
- 5 down: STEREOTYPE
- 6 down: KUROKAWA
- 7 down: JAI
- 8 down: LIST
- 9 down: PAKA
- 12 down: EAST

page 81

NIHAU
KAUAI
*Honolulu
OAHU
MOLOKAI
Pacific Ocean
LANAI
KAHOOLAWE
MAUI
Hawaii gained statehood in 1959.
HAWAII

92

GA1323